# THE SIMON & SCHUSTER
## ◈ POCKET ◈

# WINE
# LABEL
# DECODER

## ROSEMARY GEORGE
### MASTER OF WINE

◈

D0104021

**F**

A Fireside Book
Published by Simon & Schuster Inc.
New York London Toronto Sydney Tokyo Singapore

FIRESIDE
Simon & Schuster Building
Rockefeller Center
1230 Avenue of the Americas
New York, New York 10020

This edition first published in Great Britain in 1989
exclusively for Marks & Spencer p.l.c.
by arrangement with Mitchell Beazley International Ltd.

Published in Great Britain in 1990
by Mitchell Beazley International Ltd.,
Artists House, 14-15 Manette Street,
London W1V 5LB

Editor Rachel Grenfell
Art Editor Kelly Flynn
Production Stewart Bowling
Senior Executive Editor Chris Foulkes
Maps and illustrations by Isobel Balakristnan

Printed and bound in Hong Kong
Origination by Scantrans in Singapore

10 9 8 7 6 5 4 3 2

Library of Congress Cataloging in Publication Data
available upon request

ISBN: 0-671-72897-0

# CONTENTS

# INTRODUCTION

*A* wine label provides a key. It tells us what wine is in the bottle and where it comes from. But it also does more than that. Deliberately (or sometimes subconsciously) its design conveys an impression. The label is our first point of contact with the bottle. On the wine merchant's shelf it aims to say: 'Buy me; drink me! This is what I taste like.'

The classic, elegant design of a claret label leads us to think of a serious wine with stature. On the other hand a cheerful colourful label automatically implies a simpler wine.

However, this is not always the case. Some producers attach more importance to the appearance of their bottles, others merely accept whatever their local printer offers them. At Château Simone in Provence they first began bottling their wine in the early 1920s, and more than sixty years later they see no reason to change the original label. The ultimate in sophistication is at Château Mouton Rothschild where a famous contemporary artist is commissioned each year to design the label. Works by Picasso, Chagall, and so on, are collectors' pieces.

A wine label may be there to seduce us into buying, but its prime purpose is to tell us just what is in the bottle. Certain information should be clearly visible on the label, such as the country of origin, the quality, the kind of wine and the alcoholic degree. Also there will be the name of the producer, bottler, or importer responsible for the contents of the bottle. This may sound straightforward, but wine labels have developed a jargon of their own, which to the inexperienced may seem meaningless. The reason for this book then is to provide a way through the maze of label terminology.

# READING A LABEL

*W*hat makes one wine different from another? There are four essential elements that determine the taste of a wine: grape variety, the soil in which it is grown, the climate to which it is subjected each year, and finally the human factor, the winemaker.

Two of these elements are constant, namely the grape variety and the soil. These are evident in the name of the wine. For instance, if you see Beaujolais on a label, this tells you that you have a wine made from the Gamay grape, grown on granite soil. Chablis implies Chardonnay grown on clay and limestone. Sometimes the grape variety forms part of the wine name, such as Riesling d'Alsace or Bulgarian Cabernet Sauvignon, but more often than not a certain amount of knowledge is assumed. This is, of course, frustrating to the newcomer to wine, but knowledge comes with experience and tasting.

The third element is the climate, which is part constant, part variable. By virtue of its situation Burgundy in northern France enjoys a cooler climate than say Jumilla in southern Spain. You can therefore expect Burgundy to produce wines which are lighter, with more acidity and less alcohol than Jumilla, which, coming from the warm south, lack acidity and are fullbodied, heady and alcoholic.

The further north in the northern hemisphere, or south in the southern hemisphere a vineyard is located, the greater the annual variations in climate. Grapes grown on the edge of the climatic boundaries have in fine years an intensity of flavour which is not possible in sunsoaked vineyards with little variation of climate, but when the weather is unkind, unripe grapes make thin, insipid wine. The greater the climatic differences, the more importance needs to be attached to the vintage date.

There are numerous wines, such as Liebfraumilch, Muscadet, Vinho Verde, etc., for which the vintage is relatively unimportant, except that they should be drunk as young as possible. Check that you are buying a wine which is no more than a year or so old. Another example of a vintage being unimportant is blended wines such as sherry, port and champagne. You never see a vintage date on a bottle of sherry. Champagne is usually a blend of a number of years and only sometimes sold as a vintage wine. Port is only sold with a vintage in years of exceptional quality.

The vintage is of utmost significance when you buy fine wines, such as classed growth claret, Italian riservas, or German Spätlese. Here the quality and staying power can vary considerably with the climatic changes from year to year. This is the reason for using vintage charts as quick and easy guides to annual variations, although inevitably there are always exceptions in every year.

In between the two extremes there are the instances when a vintage matters sometimes. An example might be Beaujolais, for which the normal choice would be the most recent vintage, except in the years when an exceptionally good wine is made.

The final element in determining the taste of a wine is the human factor, the winemaker. A skilled and conscientious winemaker can produce something palatable out of less than perfect grapes and redeem a bad harvest by careful vinification. On the other hand a careless winemaker can ruin healthy ripe grapes to make undrinkable wine.

In some regions such as Burgundy, where vineyards are often divided between several different people, the winemaker's name on the label is of considerable importance, even to the extent of differentiating between Christian names with the same surname. This may be the clue to an outstanding wine or to a wine which is best avoided. The only way through this minefield is to write down and remember the names of producers whose wines you have enjoyed.

Names may appear on the label other than the winemaker's. On a bottle of burgundy you may find the name of the merchant or négociant élèveur who has bought newly fermented wine from a grower (or possibly grapes or unfermented juice) which is then treated, matured and prepared for bottling. Alternatively a négociant may bottle the wine of several small growers who do not have the necessary facilities. If they are skilled, very good wines result and buyers come to rely on the négociant's name.

Sometimes the producer's or merchant's name may be insignificant since it is the brand name, such as Blue Nun or Mateus Rosé, which counts. A brand has the advantage of offering a constant taste. That is its aim, to produce a regular consistent flavour upon which the consumer can rely.

Wine merchants' or supermarket names may feature on the label of what are commonly called 'own label' wines. They encourage consumers to place their confidence in that merchant's expertise in choosing wine.

The names on the label give you the clue as to where the wine has been between the producer's cellar and your dining table. The chain may be very short – from winemaker to wine merchant. Or the wine may have been made by a small grower, sold to a larger company for bottling, then sold to the importer, who in turn has your wine merchant as a customer. The bottler's name must always appear on the label, while an importer's name must also feature for countries outside the Common Market.

It is not necessary for a wine to be bottled at its place of origin, although this is a growing trend. Traditional English wine merchants created a reputation for their own bottlings of claret and port, but it is now obligatory for all classed growth claret and vintage port to be bottled in Bordeaux and Oporto.

Some appellations, such as Alsace, demand that the wine is bottled within the appellation. Terms like 'mis en bouteille au château' or 'mis au domaine' tell you the wine is estate bottled.

Considerable effort is put into the design of wine labels. After all, it is the appearance of the label which first encourages you to pick the bottle from the shelf. An elegant label for an Italian vino da tavola may tell you that more importance is placed on the 'alternative wine' than on the DOC. On the other hand, an elegant label for indifferent contents is obviously intended to camouflage the mediocrity of the bottle.

There are some expressions used on wine labels which make a wine seem more prestigious than it actually is. One example is Blanc de Blancs which means, literally, white wine made from white grapes. In fact all white wine, with the exception of some sparkling wines, is made from white grapes, so there is nothing special about it at all. The word 'château' is commonly associated with Bordeaux, and again sounds prestigious, although the château in question may only be a rundown farmhouse. Nor is it the prerogative of Bordeaux. You can find château as part of the name of any appellation wine, though never of vins de pays; the word even features in wine names in Australia and California. The word cru is often qualified by grand. In the Médoc part of Bordeaux this means something, telling you the château is one of the classified growths of the region. In contrast, in St-Emilion, where there are numerous undistinguished grands crus, it is of little significance. In Provence cru classé on the label is purely historical, while in Switzerland grand cru is a product of the producer's imagination, without any foundation.

Apart from the main label on the body of the bottle, you may also find a neck label and even a back label. The neck label will often give you the vintage date, while the back label may provide you with extra optional information about the wine.

Sometimes you can even learn about the wine from the capsule (the covering over the cork). The most notable example of this is the fine German estate of Schloss Vollrads, whose capsules are colour coded according to the taste and particularly the sweetness level of the wine. The label will substantiate this with the Prädikat and the colour of the capsule. For example, a blue capsule is for Kabinett; a silver band means the wine is dry, and a gold one that it is sweet. Colour codings, looking rather like bus tickets, also appear on South African bottles to substantiate the information on the label.

In Spain and Portugal the growers' association in each area guarantees the authenticity of the wine with a seal on the label or a band over the cork under the capsule. The paper seal breaks only when you open the bottle. In Italy bottles of Chianti Classico often carry a black cockerel on the capsule to show that the producers belong to the voluntary quality control organization of the Gallo Nero.

One of the problems in choosing a wine is knowing whether a white wine will be sweet or dry, or a red wine heavy or light. Occasionally, where there are variations within the appellation or DOC, the label will tell you with words like moelleux, brut or dolce, but often the poor consumer is expected to know. Therefore the Wine Development Board, the organization which promotes wine in general, irrespective of its country of origin, has tried to help by developing a scale of sweetness which it encourages supermarkets and wine merchants to use. It has graded all white wines from one to nine (dry to sweet), with symbols which some merchants are using on their wine labels and others use on shelf labels. EEC regulations allow this grading of white wines to appear on the label, but unfortunately do not permit the coding of red wines. Consequently the grading of red wines according to their weight from A to E (light to heavy) has been less successful.

# WINE LAWS

*A* wine label's main purpose is to tell the consumer just what it is he or she is buying. This means that the label must describe the contents of the bottle accurately and legally.

As a member of the Common Market, Great Britain conforms to EEC labelling regulations and must accept the provisions laid down by the member wine-producing countries for their producers. Remember the Spanish Chablis and Spanish Sauternes we all drank before 1973? It would now be illegal to use terms like Chablis except on the real thing. Wine labels in this country are now controlled by the Wine Standards Board, a watchdog body, whose inspectors keep a sharp lookout for any malpractices.

EEC wine law divides what it calls 'light still wine' (as opposed to sparkling or fortified wine) into three broad categories for wine produced within the Common Market. These are table wine, table wine entitled to a geographic name and quality wine produced in a specified region. France, Italy, Germany, Spain and Portugal all recognize these distinct categories.

Suffice it to say the appropriate quality must appear on the label. Taking France as an example, the label will include appellation contrôlée or vin délimité de qualité supérieure, both of which are quality wines produced in a specified region, or vin de pays, which is a table wine entitled to a geographic name, or simple vin de table.

For some bureaucratic reason, countries outside the Common Market are required to have only two categories: the basic quality of wine which is simply called wine, rather than table wine, and wine entitled to a geographic name. Portugal, a recent member of the Common Market, is still enjoying a period of transition and her wines may be labelled like third country wines until the end of 1990.

The label must carry the name and address of the person or company responsible for the contents of the bottle. Legally this is the bottler who may, of course, also be the producer. However, if they are two different people or companies, you will find words to that effect: 'bottled by X for Y'. In the case of a fine quality wine, the name of the producer is boldly proclaimed on the label, while a mere table wine carries a name and postal code in the smallest permitted print size. The size of lettering for obligatory information on wine bottles is strictly controlled, and the Wine Standards Board inspectors have accurate rulers. If a wine has been bottled outside the EEC, the importer's name must also appear. The country of origin is essential, whatever the category of the wine.

The bottle size is compulsory. The Common Market has encouraged a certain conformity in bottle sizes, rationalizing some of the more esoteric sizes such as 73 or 68 centilitres. It has succeeded in whittling them down to 70 and 75 centilitres, but from the beginning of 1989, 75 centilitres became the standard legal size. Half bottles now contain 37.5 centilitres and a magnum 150 centilitres. The litre size is also allowed, and so is the much less common 50 centilitre bottle, the 2 litre bottle, and multiples of 75 centilitres for giant bottles of champagne.

One or two traditional anomalies remain. Vin Jaune from the Jura is sold in the *clavelin* bottle of 62 centilitres for the historical reason that after the mandatory six years ageing period in cask 100 litres of Vin Jaune will be reduced by evaporation to 62 litres. Bottle sizes are usually measured in centilitres expressed as 75 cl. or in millilitres, as 750 ml. On some labels the letter 'e' next to the bottle size used to mean the bottle was an authorized size. This is now defunct.

Since May 1988 it has been obligatory to mention the alcohol content of a wine. However, labels already printed before that date are allowed to be used up. Alcohol is usually measured as a percentage by volume and may read, for example, as 11° or 11%. It must be accurate to within half a degree.

On the subject of additives, sulphur dioxide is one which has attracted the most attention. It is commonly used in wine making and has been so for centuries. It is an antiseptic and also prevents oxidation. Without it wine would soon turn to vinegar. Virtually all wines contain some. Levels are strictly controlled, and some labels, especially those from Australia and the United States say so, with the words, 'contains sulphites' or mention the E number 220.

Labelling regulations are designed to prevent a wine from sounding better than it actually is. Consequently, many of the words which have connotations of quality are not allowed in the description of a basic table wine. Only a colour and a flavour are permitted.

Once a geographical origin is mentioned, more information is allowed, such as a grape variety, an estate name and a vintage. However, words such as grand vin, cuvée speciale and so on, are closely controlled. In France, a vin de pays must never be from a château, only a domaine, even if there is the finest, medieval château on the property.

Once the wine is recognized as a quality wine there is even greater flexibility about what is allowed on the label. The area of origin must be given, which may be as precise as a part of a single vineyard. A considerable number of different quality terms are allowed, as diverse as grand vin, vin fin, grand cru, superiore, vergine, extra, vinho de qualidade, some of which mean something quite specific, and others nothing at all. The regulations include a long list, but anything not actually permitted as an optional extra is forbidden.

# INTRODUCTION
# TO FRANCE

*F*rench wine law hangs upon the importance of the precise origins of the grapes that make a wine. The winemakers of France also believe that some vineyards make very much better wine than others by virtue of their soil. The composition of the soil may change from one side of a valley or hillside to another, and with it the status of the vineyard. Altitude, the way the ground slopes, and microclimate are also important.

Consequently the French appellations dictate exactly what grapes may be grown where, in accordance with traditional customs. A precise survey of vineyards has been carried out, which clearly defines the boundaries of the appellation.

The first appellations were created in 1936, born of the need to take steps against widespread fraud in the French wine trade between the two world wars. The first appellation came from Châteauneuf-du-Pape, where Baron le Roy of Château Fortia worked out, among other things, that Châteauneuf-du-Pape could only be properly produced from land where lavender and thyme grew. Thus soil was immediately of prime importance. As well as delimiting the vineyard area, an appellation lays down the grape varieties that may be planted, the maximum amount of grapes they may produce, the way the vines may be pruned and, often, precise wine making techniques. All this is strictly controlled by the Institut d'Appellations d'Origine.

The category of appellation contrôlée covers only 28 per cent of the total French wine production and includes the country's best wines. A more recent creation is the much smaller category of Vins Délimités de Qualité Supérieure (VDQS), which covers second rank appellations and accounts for a minute 1.3 per cent of the country's wine. The regulations governing these wines are also strict.

The newest sector of French wines are the vins de pays, a term which translates literally as 'country wine'. These were born out of the urgent need to find a remedy for the vast 'wine lake' of overproduction in the south of France; wine without character of quality.

A vin de pays is considered to be a superior vin de table and comes from a specific area. In nearly all cases these areas are determined by administrative boundaries. The regulations are not as strict as for an appellation or a VDQS, but they do allow for experimentation which is not possible in more traditional appellations. Vins de pays can encompass some of the best and the worst of French wine making.

The fourth and largest category, vin de table, is the least important. These are the everyday wines sold under a brand name, but with little further indication of provenance and often not even bottled.

# BORDEAUX

*S*ome of the greatest red wines of the world, which in England are traditionally called claret, come from Bordeaux. So do the best sweet white and some exceptional dry white wines. This makes Bordeaux a contender for the world's greatest wine region.

Let us take red wine first and explain the appellations and terms that appear on the label and determine the choice of a bottle. The simplest and most basic appellation is **Bordeaux** which covers the whole of the département of the Gironde. Such a wine may simply be described as a 'house claret' by a wine merchant or supermarket. If it has an extra half degree of alcohol, it is called **Bordeaux Supérieur**. The vineyards of Bordeaux are divided into châteaux and some 7,000 such estates are identified in Bordeaux's massive reference book, *Féret*. An estate name nearly always includes the word château, but domaine or clos are sometimes used and have the same meaning. Literally the term château translates as a castle, but in practice it may either be a smart country house or, more likely, a simple farmhouse.

The heart of fine claret lies in the Médoc. This is the home of all but one of the sixty-one châteaux that were recognized as crus classés (classed growths) in 1855, coming mainly from four principal villages or communes which are appellations in their own right, namely **St-Estèphe**, **Pauillac**, **Margaux** and **St-Julien**. In addition there are the two outlying villages of **Moulis** and **Listrac**. There is also the appellation of **Haut Médoc**, which includes the vineyards surrounding these six villages but which are not part of their appellations. The appellation **Médoc** covers an area originally known as Bas Médoc to the north of the Haut Médoc. Bordeaux, it seems, is very class conscious for, in addition to the wines of the 1855 classification (which are split into 5 categories), there is an infrastructure of cru bourgeois, cru grand bourgeois and cru grand bourgeois exceptionnel. The latest classification of these was in 1978. A cru bourgeois is an estate of not less than seven hectares, making wine at the château of sufficient quality to qualify as a member of the association of cru bourgeois. A cru *grand* bourgeois must also age its wine in oak barrels, while a cru grand bourgeois *exceptionnel* comes only from the Haut Médoc and must bottle its wine at the château.

On the right bank of the Gironde there is the picturesque town of **St-Emilion**, with a handful of surrounding 'satellite' appellations: **Montagne**, **St-Georges**, **Lussac**, and **Puisseguin**, each hyphenated to the name St-Emilion. The wines from these are similar to St-Emilion but lighter. St-Emilion is classified too, but only since 1958, into premier grands crus, grand cru classé and grand cru. Premier grand cru singles out Ausone and Cheval Blanc as class A and nine others as class B. In theory the classification is supposed to be revised every ten years, with appropriate promotions and demotions. The last occasion was in 1985, when some minor changes took place including the controversial demotion of one premier grands crus. There are now sixty-two grands crus classés.

Adjoining St-Emilion are the vineyards of **Pomerol** which until about twenty years ago was a small sleepy backwater far from the mainstream of Bordeaux. It is now the appellation of one of the world's most expensive red wines, Château Pétrus, generally considered to be of first growth quality. However, unlike the other main areas of Bordeaux, Pomerol has never been given an official classification. **Lalande de Pomerol** is a satellite appellation, like those around St-Emilion.

The third significant red appellation of Bordeaux is the **Graves**, although since 1987 the better châteaux come under the new appellation of **Pessac–Léognan**: similar to the Graves, but limited to the ten best villages. The Graves is one of the very few Bordeaux appellations that can be both red and white. There is a separate classification for each colour, made as recently as 1953. However Château Haut Brion is the one estate outside the Médoc to feature in the 1855 classification. Thirteen châteaux can use the term cru classé for their red wine and nine for their white wine. Some names feature in both lists.

It is the blend of grape varieties, combined with the soil of the vineyards, that determine the different flavours of claret. In the Médoc, where the soil is very gravelly, Cabernet Sauvignon is the dominant grape variety, blended with some Cabernet Franc and Merlot. In St-Emilion and Pomerol, where there is more clay and sand, Merlot is the principal grape, blended more with Cabernet Franc than Cabernet Sauvignon. The wines of the Graves are similar to those of the Médoc. The differences come through in the taste, so that wines from the Médoc

*Compare Château Latour and Château de la Tour – two wines with very similar names and both from Bordeaux, but look at the difference.*

### Château Latour
*Château Latour's is a much more elegant and prestigious looking label, as is the wine.*

*The great or best wine of the estate. A term that may not necessarily mean anything specific, but in this instance refers to the fact that Château Latour produces a second wine, Les Forts de Latour, from younger vines and any wine that is not of sufficient quality for inclusion in the grand vin.*

*Bottled at the château.*

*Its classification as a first growth in 1855.*

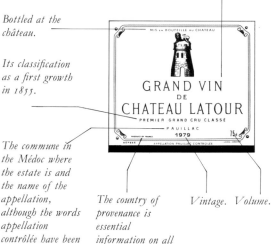

*The commune in the Médoc where the estate is and the name of the appellation, although the words appellation contrôlée have been omitted.*

*The country of provenance is essential information on all wine labels.*

*Vintage. Volume.*

possess a firm streak of tannin, with flavours reminiscent of cedarwood and blackcurrants, while those of St-Emilion and Pomerol are fuller and richer. The Graves wines can be distinguished from those of the Médoc by a typical earthy character.

The great names of Bordeaux are inevitably expensive, but good value wines are to be found among the host of so-called petits châteaux, the lesser known estates which appear in a competent

**Château de la Tour**

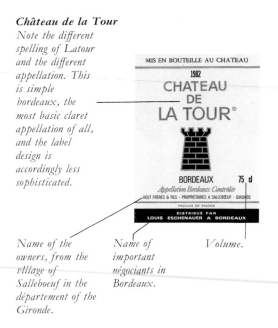

*Note the different spelling of Latour and the different appellation. This is simple bordeaux, the most basic claret appellation of all, and the label design is accordingly less sophisticated.*

*Name of the owners, from the village of Salleboeuf in the département of the Gironde.*

*Name of important négociants in Bordeaux.*

*Volume.*

wine merchant's list. These come from the outlying areas of the Gironde, from the vineyards around **Bourg** and **Blaye**, as well as from the **Premières Côtes de Bordeaux**, the **Côtes de Castillon**, **Fronsac**, **Canon–Fronsac** and the little known **Côtes de Francs**. These estates do not command high prices but can produce wines that taste better than their price would indicate.

The best dry white wines of Bordeaux come from the Graves, where a blend of Sémillon, Sauvignon and a drop of Muscadelle can produce wines with character and flavour. White Bordeaux has had a rather tarnished reputation, especially the appellation of **Entre Deux Mers**. But today the less well-known estates of the Graves and Entre Deux Mers are making some good crisp, full, dry white wines, based on the Sauvignon grape.

Within the Graves there is an enclave of sweet wine, with the twin appellations of **Sauternes** and

## St-Emilion

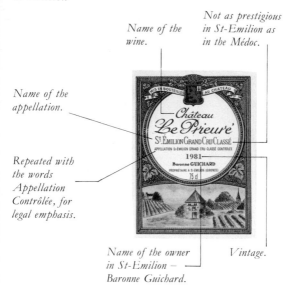

Name of the wine.

Not as prestigious in St-Emilion as in the Médoc.

Name of the appellation.

Repeated with the words Appellation Contrôlée, for legal emphasis.

Name of the owner in St-Emilion – Baronne Guichard.

Vintage.

**Barsac**. A Barsac estate may put Sauternes .on its label, but never vice versa. The quality of these wines depends upon the development of a fungus, *Botrytis cinerea*, commonly called 'noble rot', which only occurs when the climatic conditions are right. These are damp misty autumnal mornings, followed by brilliant sunshine. The humidity encourages the development of the fungus on the ripening grapes while the warm sunshine dries them, causing dehydration. Their juice becomes sweet and concentrated and turns into rich luscious wine. Barsac is very similar in taste to Sauternes, perhaps a hint lighter and more lemony.

In 1855, twenty-four Sauternes châteaux were recognized as premiér (1er) cru classé and deuxième (2me) cru classé. Yquem is indisputably considered the best of them. Because it is difficult to make a living from sweet wines alone, many of these estates also produce a dry wine such as Ygrec and R de Rieussec, which at least gives them a more certain

## Sauterns

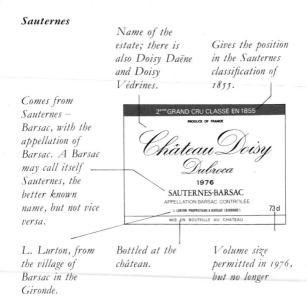

Name of the estate; there is also Doisy Daëne and Doisy Védrines.

Gives the position in the Sauternes classification of 1855.

Comes from Sauternes – Barsac, with the appellation of Barsac. A Barsac may call itself Sauternes, the better known name, but not vice versa.

L. Lurton, from the village of Barsac in the Gironde.

Bottled at the château.

Volume size permitted in 1976, but no longer

income. The appellation of these dry whites is not Sauternes or Barsac but simple Bordeaux Blanc.

There are other peripheral areas which make acceptable sweet wine in good years, such as **Ste-Croix du Mont**, **Loupiac**, **Cérons** and **Cadillac**. Often these wines are made from overripe rather than nobly rotten grapes. The good can provide excellent drinking value, but the bad are over-sulphured and a certain recipe for a headache. Sometimes it may not be apparent whether a white Bordeaux is sweet or dry. A guideline is the colour of the bottle; sweet wines always comes in clear glass bottles and dry wines generally in green.

# BURGUNDY

*T*he vineyards of Burgundy divide into five distinct regions. Travelling south they are **Chablis**, the Côte d'Or, Côte Chalonnaise, **Beaujolais** and Mâconnais.

The grape variety for all Chablis, and indeed all fine white burgundy, is Chardonnay. The vineyards of Chablis split into four qualities. The least important is **Petit Chablis**, next is Chablis and finally the various vineyards which are designated as premiers and grands crus. The grand cru vineyards, reckoned the best, are grouped together on one prime hillside just outside the town, with seven vineyard names which appear on a label along with 'Grand Cru'. The premiers crus are more complicated because there are more than thirty possible names, although some of them have been grouped together under the more popular umbrella names. For example, a grower may bottle wine as L'Homme Mort, or sell it under the better known name of Fourchaume, a premier cru which includes the vineyards of L'Homme Mort and other premiers crus.

Simple Chablis is a firm, dry white wine, with fruit to balance the acidity. From a good grower it offers a deliciously dry flinty glass of wine. Premier cru Chablis will have a little more weight, while the quality of grand cru Chablis can rival wines from further south, but always with the firm bite of acidity that comes from a northern vineyard. Sometimes these better wines are fermented, or aged, in oak barrels, which gives them a little more substance. Good Chablis is never cheap for it suffers from the climatic extremes of a northern vineyard.

Traditionally a large proportion of Chablis was, and still is, sold by merchants from the Côte d'Or or Beaujolais. Many of these use secondary names or *sous marques*. Should the producer's name be unfamiliar, his address on the label will reveal if the wine has been to Beaune or Mâcon before first crossing the Channel or the Atlantic.

Nearby villages outside the appellation of Chablis, such as **Irancy**, **Coulanges-la-Vineuse** and **Epineuil**, make some interesting red wines. They are not often exported but worth seeking out. **Sauvignon de St-Bris**, from the village of St-Bris-le-Vineux, is an anomaly because it is a VDQS which can never be promoted to an appellation since Sauvignon is not considered to be a Burgundian grape variety.

The vineyards of the Côte d'Or are some hundred miles further south from Chablis. This is the heart of Burgundy, the home of some of the greatest red wines of France, for red Burgundy when good is sublime. The key to quality is the name of the producer on the label, a factor which applies throughout Burgundy. French inheritance laws have meant that many vineyards have been divided up into small parcels, so that several people may own one small vineyard, each making wine in their individual way, giving the consumer as many wines as makers to choose between. The ultimate example of this is **Clos Vougeot**, a fifty hectare vineyard with no less than eighty-five owners. The confusion is such that one day you may drink a Clos Vougeot which you like, while the next disappoints, even though it is the same vintage. The answer lies in the producer's name on the label. Never buy a wine from Burgundy without knowing who made it.

The Côte d'Or divides into two, the **Côte de Nuits** and the **Côte de Beaune**. The first makes almost exclusively red wine, while the second also produces some of the world's greatest white wine. The better vineyards of each village are recognized as premiers crus and even better grands crus. Historically the best vineyard of the village has been hyphenated with the village name. **Aloxe-Corton** is one such example, for Corton is quite the best red wine of the village of Aloxe. Vineyard names feature on the label with their status which tells you if an unknown vineyard is a premier cru. If it just says premier cru, without a vineyard name, the wine is a blend from several premiers crus vineyards in the village.

There are also several basic Burgundy appellations. **Bourgogne blanc** and **Bourgogne rouge**, pure Chardonnay and Pinot Noir respectively, are at the bottom of the scale, but from a reputable grower can offer very good value, with wine better than the label would indicate. **Bourgogne Passe-tous-grains** is a blend of a minimum one-third Pinot Noir with Gamay. **Bourgogne Grand Ordinaire** comes in both red and white, and is usually more ordinary than grand. The red is generally Gamay, and the white Sacy or Aligoté. Better Aligoté comes within the appellation **Bourgogne Aligoté**, for a crisp dry

## *Chablis*

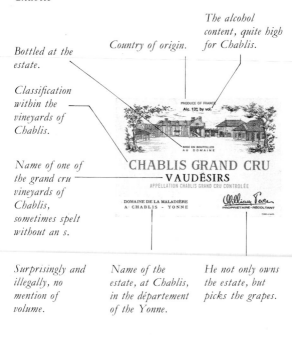

The alcohol content, quite high for Chablis.

Country of origin.

Bottled at the estate.

Classification within the vineyards of Chablis.

Name of one of the grand cru vineyards of Chablis, sometimes spelt without an s.

**PRODUCE OF FRANCE**
Alc. 13% by vol.

MISE EN BOUTEILLE
AU DOMAINE

**CHABLIS GRAND CRU**
**VAUDÉSIRS**
APPELLATION CHABLIS GRAND CRU CONTRÔLÉE

DOMAINE DE LA MALADIÈRE
A CHABLIS - YONNE

PROPRIÉTAIRE - RÉCOLTANT

Surprisingly and illegally, no mention of volume.

Name of the estate, at Chablis, in the département of the Yonne.

He not only owns the estate, but picks the grapes.

Vintage must be on a neck label.

white wine which is mixed with a drop of cassis to make the traditional Burgundian aperitif Kir Cassis. **Bourgogne Aligoté Bouzeron** is the only appellation indicating the provenance of the Aligoté grape as from that village. Otherwise your clue is the grower's address; some of the best come from St-Bris-le-Vineux.

The Côte d'Or includes the peripheral appellations of the **Hautes Côtes de Nuits** and the **Hautes Côtes de Beaune** which, as their names imply, come from behind the main slopes. In good years, such as 1985, they offer good value, ripe wines. In bad years they are thin and acid and should be avoided.

Potential confusion lies in the names of the

### Bourgogne Pinot Noir

*A burgundy made from Pinot Noir; unusual in giving the grape variety, the name of which is not included in the appellation.*

*Bottled at the property.*

*A fancy, decorative term, but of no specific meaning, other than conveying the producer's own opinion of his wine.*

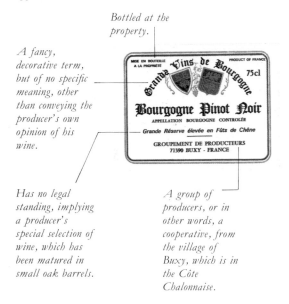

*Has no legal standing, implying a producer's special selection of wine, which has been matured in small oak barrels.*

*A group of producers, or in other words, a cooperative, from the village of Buxy, which is in the Côte Chalonnaise.*

appellations of **Côte de Beaune** and **Côte de Beaune Villages**. The first applies only to a few vineyards around the town of Beaune, while the second covers red wines mainly from the villages known above all for their white wines. In complete contrast **Côtes de Nuits Villages** covers red and white wines from the lesser known villages of the Côtes de Nuits.

Bargains are rare in Burgundy, but if you are lucky, you may unearth one in the Côte Chalonnaise, also known as the Région de Mercurey. This area is divided into four main villages, each with an appellation, namely **Givry**, **Mercurey**, **Montagny** and **Rully**. The first two are mainly red, while Montagny is only white and Rully both. Montagny premier cru indicates nothing more than a higher level of alcohol, a minimum 11.5°, and can include all the vineyards of the village, while Rully premier cru applies only to certain named vineyards.

The simplest and most unassuming burgundy of all is Beaujolais. The difference lies in the grape variety, which is Gamay rather than Pinot Noir. Vinification methods are different too, whereas Pinot Noir is destalked and fermented in the classic manner, whole bunches of Gamay are put into the closed fermentation vat and the carbon dioxide from that fermentation retained until the grapes are pressed. The result is a fresh easy-to-drink wine, with more fruit than tannin. Most popular of all Beaujolais is Beaujolais Nouveau, which appears on the third Thursday of November and can be described as Nouveau until Christmas. However, in a good year it may well taste better at Easter. Other appellations have followed the example of Beaujolais, so that you can now find Gaillac Nouveau, and so on. The attraction is a successful marketing gimmick rather than any concept of quality. But the wine, in a good year, can be fun. The basic appellation is Beaujolais which covers a large area between Mâcon and Lyons. **Beaujolais Villages** covers a smaller area of thirty-eight better villages, whose names may appear on the label, while the best Beaujolais of all comes from the ten crus, each with their own appellation, such as **Moulin à Vent**, **Juliénas**, **Fleurie**, and most recently **Regnié**. Mention should also be made of the adjoining but little known **Côteaux du Lyonnais**, which offers excellent value for the quaffable fruity taste of Gamay.

The beautiful hills northwest of **Mâcon** produce both red and white wine, but they are better known for their whites. Red Mâcon is usually made from Gamay, but is not as attractive as simple Beaujolais. White Mâcon is made from Chardonnay and can provide excellent drinking value. **Mâcon Villages** includes forty-two villages, some of whose names

### Puligny–Montrachet

Name of the village.
Montrachet is the very best vineyard of the village. The tradition of hyphenating this to the village name has been followed.

A first growth of the village of Puligny-Montrachet.

From the estate of the Duc of Magenta, a reputable producer of burgundy.

Name of the vineyard, classified as a premier cru.

The quality of the wine.

Self-explanatory.

Bottled at the estate of the abbey of Morgeot, the name of the Duc of Magenta's estate in the adjoining village of Chassagne–Montrachet in the Côte d'Or.

Volume.

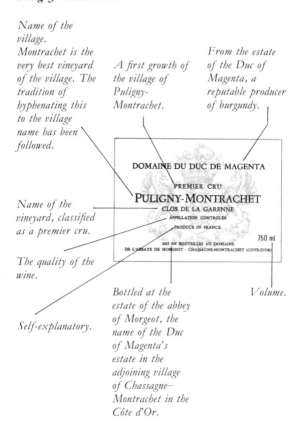

appear on the label, such as **Lugny**, **Classé** and **Prissé**. In addition there are four separate appellations, the best known of which is **Pouilly Fuissé**; the wine may be good, but its popularity on the American market is such that there is not enough to go round and so the value is bad. Better are the two satellite appellations of **Pouilly Vinzelles** and the less common **Pouilly Loché**, as well as **St-Véran** which overlaps the Mâconnais and the Beaujolais. You can find Beaujolais blanc but it is rare; growers prefer to use the name St-Véran. Traditionally Burgundian merchants or négociants included wines from the whole of Burgundy as well as those of the Rhône valley in their repertoire. It is only in recent years that the smaller individual growers of Burgundy have begun to bottle their own wines and create their own reputations. A négociant usually provides a certain consistency of quality, while a grower may offer some of the greatest wines of the region or, if his cellar is badly equipped, some of the worst. The range of quality, especially for red burgundy, is phenomenal because the Pinot Noir is so very difficult to grow and vinify.

# THE JURA

*M*ountains lend themselves to individuality and so the isolated position of the Jura, right on the border with Switzerland, produces wines which are not quite like anything else from the rest of France. There are four appellations, making a variety of colours. **Château-Chalon** is the most individual as it allows only for Vin Jaune, a curiously oxidized wine that develops *flor* like fino sherry. Vin Jaune is also found in the other appellations of the Jura. **Arbois**, from around the town of the same name, covers red, white and pink wine as well. **L'Etoile**, so-called after the star shaped fossils in the soil, makes white and yellow wine, while the **Côtes du Jura**, which covers all those vineyards not included in the other three appellations, makes all colours of wine. Champagne method sparkling wine is also produced with some success.

The principal grape varieties of the Jura are not found anywhere else in France. Savagnin, which may be related to the Gewürztraminer of Alsace, makes Vin Jaune. Chardonnay is also grown for white wine, as is Pinot Noir for reds, but it is Trousseau and Poulsard which give the red and pink wines of the Jura their character. The pinks are fuller bodied than is usual for pink wines, while the reds are lighter and more perfumed. The tastes are quite unique.

Another curiosity is Vin de Paille, which translates literally as 'straw wine', made originally by drying the grapes on straw until they became shrivelled and dehydrated. The resulting wine is sweet and rich, an unusual but delicious dessert wine.

### Côtes du Jura

*The name of the estate, with a long history as the foot of the label tells you. That is very*

*much optional information and could equally well appear on a back label.*

*Colour of the wine; Côtes du Jura can be red, white, pink or coral, and even yellow.*

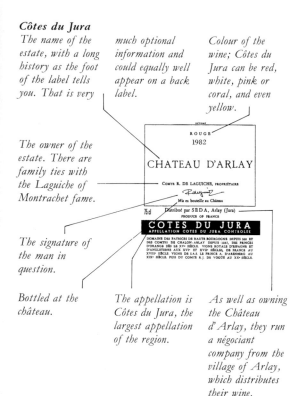

*The owner of the estate. There are family ties with the Laguiche of Montrachet fame.*

*The signature of the man in question.*

*Bottled at the château.*

*The appellation is Côtes du Jura, the largest appellation of the region.*

*As well as owning the Château d'Arlay, they run a négociant company from the village of Arlay, which distributes their wine.*

# SAVOIE AND BUGEY

*T*he wines of Savoie are covered by the basic appellation **Vin de Savoie**, which has a total of sixteen crus, many of which never appear on a label. The most important are **Abymes**, **Apremont**, **Chautagne**, **Chignin** and **Ripaille**. Most of these are white, made either from the Jacquère grape, grown around Chambéry, or from the Chasselas, grown closer to Switzerland, around lake Geneva. Light red wines are made from Gamay and Pinot Noir as well as Mondeuse, which is not found anywhere else in France. Sometimes the grape variety is mentioned on the label.

In addition there are the appellations of **Crépy**, for soft, dry white wine from the Chasselas grape; **Seyssel**, which can be still or sparkling, and **Roussette de Savoie**. Roussette is a grape variety, but confusingly the appellation does not mean a wine made from that grape alone, for as much as 50 per cent Chardonnay may be blended with Roussette. Like Vin de Savoie, Roussette de Savoie has several crus, and only these are pure Roussette. However, they are rarely exported. Most Vin de Savoie is drunk locally on the ski slopes and enjoyed in the summer on the lake shores of Annecy, Geneva and Bourget.

**Vin du Bugey** is a little known VDQS made in vineyards around the town of Bellay. Like Vin de Savoie it has several crus of little importance of which Cerdon, a pink sparkling wine, is the most original. The grape variety often features on the label, which in the case of white wine is usually Chardonnay or Jacquère, while reds are made from Mondeuse, Pinot Noir or Gamay. Both reds and whites are light, fruity and dry.

## Savoie

*A pretty Alpine label, befitting to a mountain wine, with
blue gentians and the flag of Savoie.*

The appellation of
Vin de Savoie has
several crus, of
which Abymes is
one of the most
important. There
is no village;
Abymes refers to
the debris left by
a great landslide
in the 13th
century. Myans is
the nearest village.

The wine was
bottled at the
property. The
label does not say
who the proprietor
is.

The name Jean
Cavaillé is quite
prominently
displayed. He is
an important
négociant in
Savoie, who selects
several small
growers' wines for
bottling under his
own label. Hence
the words
selectionné etc. He
gives his address
of Aix-en-Savoie,
with the postal
code, and
unusually the
telephone number.

Further emphasis
of the fact that
the wine was
bottled at the
grower's cellar by
Jean Cavaillé.

# THE RHÔNE VALLEY

*T*he starting point for a journey down the Rhône valley is the city of Lyons. Travel south and you soon reach the Roman town of Vienne, with the steep vineyards of the **Côte Rôtie** on the opposite bank. The name of this appellation translates literally as the 'roasted slope' and the steep vineyards are indeed sunbaked. Here the peppery Syrah grape produces rich spicy wines that need years in bottle before they are ready for drinking. Sometimes there is mention of Côte Blonde or Côte Brune on a label when the wine comes from just one of these two slopes, but usually they are blended together.

The white wine of the northern Rhône is **Condrieu**, a deliciously fragrant wine made from the Viognier grape. The flavour is reminiscent of apricots, not firmly dry, but certainly not sweet. **Château Grillet** is a smaller, but similar appellation. Both are expensive, as the Viognier is notoriously difficult to grow, giving only very small crops, but Condrieu offers slightly better value.

A little further south are the vineyards of **Hermitage**, the other great red wine of the northern Rhône, surrounded by the larger and less distinguished appellation of **Crozes Hermitage**. Again Syrah is the grape variety and in the small vineyard of Hermitage it makes wines of great stature. Crozes Hermitage is more accessible, less long-lived, and from a good producer can give excellent value. Hermitage can also be white, from a blend of Roussanne and Marsanne, making a dry wine, which can develop interesting flavours with age.

There is no system of crus in the Rhône valley and it is rare to find individual vineyard names. Sometimes producers have adopted fantasy names for their wines. For example, one of the best Hermitage, Jaboulet's Hermitage la Chapelle, takes its name from an old chapel in the vineyards, while Chapoutier call their white Hermitage Chante Alouette. The vineyards of each appellation are owned by several people, so that, as for burgundy, the producer's name is an important consideration in the choice of wine. Like cooks, winemakers have their own particular recipes and one man's Hermitage will not be the same as another's, although the basic ingredients are identical.

Nearby **St-Joseph** is similar, but lighter, and can also be white and dry, while **Cornas**, a little to the south, makes full-flavoured peppery reds from Syrah. Its neighbour **St-Péray**, makes dry white as well as sparkling wine, from Marsanne and Rousanne.

### Rhône

Label decorated
with a rather
sober coat of
arms, recalling the
papal associations
of the wine.

Bottled at the
domaine.

Name of the
estate, and
displayed in
prominence at the
top of the label;
looks rather like
a brand name.

Wine name
displayed
prominently and
qualified by the
appellation.

Chante Cigale

MISE AU
proxies

DOMAINE
of France

Châteauneuf-du-Pape

Appellation Châteauneuf du Pape Contrôlée    75 cl e

G.A.E.C. du Domaine Chante-Cigale

JABON FAVIER  Vignerons à 84230 Châteauneuf-du-Pape (VSE), FRANCE

Name of the
estate, GAEC
stands for
Groupment
Agricole
d'Exploitation en
Commun, an
agricultural group
working together,
usually a father
and son or
daughter, or a
couple of brothers.

Name of the
producers, who
call themselves
winemakers, with
their address, the
postal code for the

village of
Châteauneuf-du-
Pape in the
département of the
Vaucluse.

The Rhône valley divides naturally into two. The
grape varieties of the north and the south are
different and between the vineyards of Cornas and
**Châteauneuf-du-Pape** there is something of a
viticultural desert. You need to take a detour east
along the river Die to find the sparkling wines of
**Clairette de Die**. South of Montélimar there is the
appellation of the **Coteaux de Tricaotin**, which is
characteristic of some of the good value drinking the
Rhône valley has to offer.

The southern Rhône means above all
Châteauneuf-du-Pape, both a red and a white wine,

from a possible thirteen different grape varieties. The white is quite full-flavoured and dry, while the red is rich, warming and fullbodied. With such a mixture of grape varieties, the taste depends much on the producer, as a considerable variation of method and style is possible. Good Châteauneuf-du-Pape, which takes its name from the summer residence of the Avignon papacy, has wonderful rich flavours; it is a wine to keep for several years.

The surrounding vineyards include the appellation of **Gigondas**, which is similar but lighter, and the much larger appellations of the **Côtes du Rhône** and **Côtes du Rhône Villages**. Côtes du Rhône is made over much of the Rhône valley, but is much more important in the south. In addition, seventeen villages have been singled out for the superior appellation of Côtes du Rhône Villages which, like Côtes du Rhône, is usually red, although white and pink wines are made too. It entails a smaller yield and higher alcohol which increases its flavour. **Cairanne** and **Vacqueyras** are generally considered to be the best of the villages, while **Beaumes-de-Venise** as well as making Côtes du Rhône Villages, has its own appellation for a vin doux naturel about which more later. Similarly **Rasteau** is both a Côtes du Rhône village and a vin doux naturel.

Nearby there is the lighter appellation of the **Côtes du Ventoux**, taking its name from the dramatic Mont Ventoux, which is mainly red, but also makes some white and pink wine. A similar appellation is the **Côtes du Vivarais**. The twin appellations of **Lirac** and **Tavel** have created a reputation for pink wine. However, Lirac now prefers to make easy-to-drink reds, while Tavel remains faithful to its vocation for dry, rather solid pinks.

In the southern Rhône the most interesting wines are red. The best offer wonderful rich, fruity flavours characteristic of the warm, sunsoaked vineyards of the south.

# THE LOIRE
# VALLEY

*T*he Loire valley is the most varied wine region in all France. The Loire rises in the rugged hills of the Massif Central and on its long journey to the Atlantic Ocean meanders past not only vineyards, but orchards, pastures and royal châteaux.

Travelling from its source the first vineyards are the twin VDQS of the **Côtes du Forez** and the **Côte Roannaise**. Gamay is the principal grape variety here. The vineyards are not so very far from Beaujolais and it is no surprise that the taste of the wines closely resembles the cheerful fruitiness of quaffable Beaujolais.

Travelling downstream the next wine area you encounter is **St-Pourçain** from around the town of the same name. The vineyards are on the banks of the river Sioule, which is a tributary of the Allier, which in turn flows into the Loire. The VDQS of St-Pourçain can be red, white and pink. White is best from a curious mixture of Sauvignon, Chardonnay and Sacy, which makes a dry, slightly nutty wine. The red comes from Pinot Noir and Gamay which makes an indifferent type of Passe-tous-grains.

It is not until you reach the town of Pouilly-sur-Loire that you meet the first serious wines of the

### Pouilly Fumé

A rather sober label, indicating a serious wine.

The vintage will be on the neck label.

Producer's family name and also the name of the company. One of the best of the appellation.

The name of the wine, repeated with the words appellation contrôlée underneath. A dry white wine made from the Sauvignon grape.

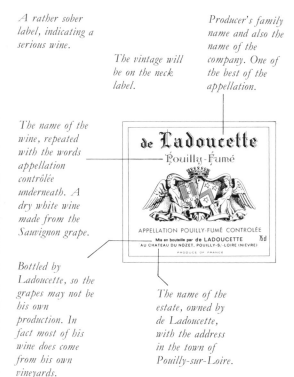

Bottled by Ladoucette, so the grapes may not be his own production. In fact most of his wine does come from his own vineyards.

The name of the estate, owned by de Ladoucette, with the address in the town of Pouilly-sur-Loire.

Loire valley, namely **Sancerre** and **Pouilly Fumé**. Rarer and less expensive are the neighbouring **Ménétou-Salon**, **Reuilly** and **Quincy**. The grapes here are Sauvignon for pungent white wine and Pinot Noir for light red and pink wines. Pouilly Fumé and Quincy are only ever white, while Ménétou-Salon, Reuilly and Sancerre, although they are best known for white wine too, can sometimes be red or pink. An ever cheaper alternative to Sancerre can be found in the appellation of **Touraine**, from Sauvignon grown in vineyards around the town of Tours.

Further into Touraine there are the white appella-

### Vouvray

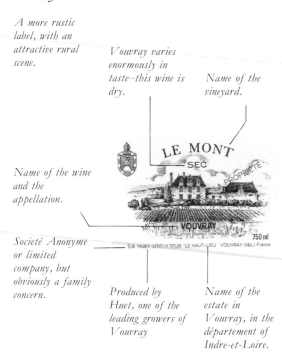

*A more rustic label, with an attractive rural scene.*

*Vouvray varies enormously in taste—this wine is dry.*

*Name of the vineyard.*

*Name of the wine and the appellation.*

*Societé Anonyme or limited company, but obviously a family concern.*

*Produced by Huet, one of the leading growers of Vouvray*

*Name of the estate in Vouvray, in the département of Indre-et-Loire.*

tions of **Vouvray** and **Montlouis**, two villages facing each other across the river. The name Vouvray on the label covers a range of flavours, for it can be still or sparkling, very dry through to very sweet. Words like sec, demi-sec, moelleux and doux provide the clue to flavour, and mousseux and the less sparkling pétillant indicate the presence of bubbles. The rarer Montlouis has the same variety of flavour and style; both are made from Chenin Blanc.

West of the town of Tours are the most serious red wines of the river, **Chinon**, **Bourgueil** and **St-Nicolas-de-Bourgueil**, which is a small enclave within the larger appellation of Bourgueil. The grape variety here is Cabernet Franc which makes delicious, fruity, easy-to-drink wines, which in better years deserve a little bottle age.

Travelling west you come to the town of **Saumur**, which is the capital of the sparkling wine industry of the Loire, about which more later. It also has an appellation for a red wine, **Saumur Champigny**, which is similar to its neighbours in Touraine.

South of the town of Angers the best sweet wines of the Loire valley are found, with the appellations of **Coteaux du Layon**, and the smaller, finer **Bonnezeaux** and **Quarts de Chaume**.

On the north side of the Loire is **Savennières**, the most individual dry white wine of the whole river. Unlike any other appellation of the Loire, Savennières includes two grands crus, **La Roche aux Moines**, and **Coulée de Serrant**. Again the grape variety is the Chenin Blanc and in Savennières it makes distinctive dry wines.

The province of Anjou is the home of **Cabernet d'Anjou** and **Rosé d'Anjou**, a pair of usually indifferent, slightly sweet pink wines. However, with the decline in the demand for this kind of pink wine, more serious producers have chosen to concentrate on their red wine to make a fruity **Anjou rouge**. The appellation of Anjou also allows for white wine. It tends to be firmly acidic, with the underlying honey taste of the Chenin Blanc.

On the Atlantic seaboard east of the city of Nantes are the vineyards of **Muscadet**, a crisp, dry white wine, made from the grape of the same name. There are three different appellations, **Muscadet**, **Muscadet des Coteaux de la Loire** and most common, **Muscadet du Sèvre et Maine**. The best Muscadet is bottled *sur lie*. Look for this on the label. Muscadet can never be a great wine. This is the fault of the grape variety, rather than the producers.

Finally, mention must be made of **Vin de Pays du Jardin de la France**, which covers the whole of the valley, and makes a cheerful basic wine.

# THE SOUTHWEST

*B*ordeaux is the starting point for the wines of southwest France, because the grape varieties which are grown for claret and Sauternes are also found in the appellations of Aquitaine. The difference becomes more marked the further you travel from the Gironde.

**Bergerac** is separated from Bordeaux by an administrative boundary. The grape varieties are identical, with Cabernet Sauvignon, Cabernet Franc and Merlot making some attractive red wines with a youthful fruitiness and a backbone of tannin. The similarity of taste is very close to that of young claret. Dry white wines are made from Sauvignon with fruity crisp flavours, while **Monbazillac** is a sweet wine made in the same way as Sauternes and its satellites. White **Côtes de Bergerac** implies a wine which is slightly sweet rather than firmly dry. Red Côtes de Bergerac has just a degree more alcohol, while **Pécharmant** is a small area, with a separate appellation, producing slightly more substantial wines than red Bergerac.

**Côtes de Duras** can be either red or white. The whites are quite crisp and dry, based on Sauvignon, while reds are rounded and fruity, again using the ·

### Bergerac

*Stylish portrayal of the château, in keeping with the tone of the label, which is elegant, and conveys an idea of a wine of some quality.*

*Name of the area of production plus the indication that the wine is dry. White Bergerac may be slightly sweet.*

*Château la Jaubertie – name of one of the leading estates of the appellation.*

*Name of the producer, who has formed a limited company. SA stands for société anonyme.*

*Qualified as always by the words appellation contrôlée.*

*Owner in the village of Colombier, in the département of the Dordogne.*

*Alcohol level.*

*Bottled at the château.*

*Contents in centilitres, followed by the 'e' mark, which is no longer necessary. It confirms that 75 cl is a legal bottle size.*

*A numbered bottle. Some wine labels tell you the total production as well.*

*In two languages, for good measure.*

## Côtes du Marmandais

*Not an appellation contrôlée, but the quality below.*

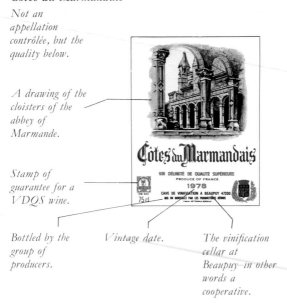

*A drawing of the cloisters of the abbey of Marmande.*

*Stamp of guarantee for a VDQS wine.*

*Bottled by the group of producers.*

*Vintage date.*

*The vinification cellar at Beaupuy—in other words a cooperative.*

grape varieties of Bordeaux. They offer good value drinking. **Côtes du Marmandais** includes Abouriou, a grape variety peculiar to that VDQS, which gives the wines a distinctive perfumed flavour.

**Buzet**—the name was changed from Côtes de Buzet with the 1988 vintage—is predominantly red and a little more substantial than Côtes de Duras.

**Cahors** in the Lot valley has more individual flavours, for this is the one wine of the southwest which does not allow any Cabernet Sauvignon. The main grape variety is the sturdy Auxerrois, or Malbec, which is blended with Tannat and Merlot. Cahors is always red, and often aged in oak. It is one of the most long-lived and individual wines of the southwest.

Further east there is the appellation of **Gaillac** which encompasses an enormous variety of flavours. Gaillac can be red, white or pink, still or sparkling, sweet or dry. A Gaillac Nouveau, made from Gamay, offers an interesting alternative to Beaujolais Nouveau. More substantial red Gaillac is based on the unusual Duras grape and, according to the producer's whim, may be blended with Cabernet and Merlot or Braucol and Syrah, or any permutation of these grape varieties. The label on white Gaillac usually says if it is dry or sec, semi-sweet or moelleux, or even sweet or doux, while **Gaillac Perlé** indicates a hint of sparkle due to the carbon dioxide remaining from the malolactic fermentation. The grape varieties here are Mauzac and Loin de l'El, and you can also find Sauvignon and Sémillon. Occasionally mention of premières côtes appears on a label. This means that the wine comes from one of eleven villages. The term is rarely used.

Nearby is an up-and-coming appellation, the **Côtes du Frontonnais**, where the distinctive Négrette grape makes wines with an individual perfumed flavour.

Closer to the Pyrenees is another substantial red wine, **Madiran**, for which the principal grape variety is Tannat blended with Merlot and Cabernet. Like many of these lesser known regions of southwest France, the quality has improved enormously in recent years and the wines offer good value for money, rich flavours with fruit and body.

The principal white wine of the Pyrenees is **Jurançon**, which is either quite dry, in which case it will be labelled sec, or slightly sweet, called moelleux by the French. The grape varieties are peculiar to the Pyrenees, mainly Gros Manseng and Petit Manseng; the wines are quite delicious. Jurancon sec has a flavour reminiscent of grapefruit. Like Alsace, it is not really austerely dry, but quite grapey, while the sweeter version is delicately honeyed. The quality is still a little variable but, as is the case all over southwest France, the wines from the better producers are much underrated and worthy of more attention.

# LANGUEDOC — ROUSSILLON

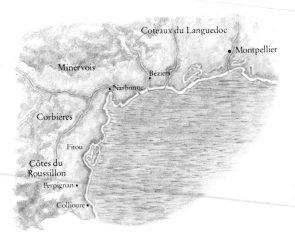

*I*n many ways this is one of the most exciting wine regions of France today, for it is an area which is undergoing a dramatic change. The region stretches from the foothills of the Pyrenees by the Spanish border through the départements of the Pyrenées-Orientales, Aude, Hérault and Gard to the mouth of the Rhône. The reputation of these vineyards was for uninspiring red plonk, without character or flavour, and which contributed to the European wine lake.

Many of the vineyards of the fertile coastal plain are disappearing as it is recognized that more exciting wines are produced from the poor soil of the foothills of the Massif Central.

Things are now changing. Vinification methods are improving enormously and there are some palatable wines to be discovered. Apart from the more traditional appellations, there are vins de pays which provide an opportunity for experimentation

47

among the more adventurous producers. Quality inevitably varies enormously, depending upon the producer. A vin de pays from the Midi may have a taste which is far superior to the name on the label, or it may come from high-yielding Carignan and Cinsaut and be devoid of all flavour. However, the greater part of the insipid characterless wines of the Midi rarely travels abroad. It tends to be the more interesting wines which find their way into bottles rather than ten-litre plastic containers.

What follows is a thumbnail sketch of the principal wines of the south, beginning by the Spanish border at Collioure and travelling east along the Mediterranean coast. The small appellation of **Collioure** is a full-bodied characterful red, forming an island of quality within the larger area of the

### Roussillon

*A simple label with a drawing of the family house.*

*Gives you the name of the estate, called after the family.*

*The appellation, a warm fruity wine from the south.*

Produit de France
1982
DOMAINE
SARDA-MALET
CÔTES du ROUSSILLON
*Appellation Côtes du Roussillon Contrôlée*
Mise en bouteille à Perpignan par
SARDA-MALET, producteurs -134 Aᵛ V.Dalbiez
66000 PERPIGNAN    75 cl

*Bottled in Perignan by Sarda Malet, who are producers at this address, in Perpignan. What was an old family house on the outskirts of Perpignan has now been engulfed by an industrial estate.*

## Vin de Pays

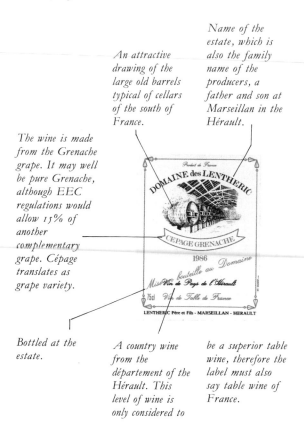

Name of the estate, which is also the family name of the producers, a father and son at Marseillan in the Hérault.

An attractive drawing of the large old barrels typical of cellars of the south of France.

The wine is made from the Grenache grape. It may well be pure Grenache, although EEC regulations would allow 15% of another complementary grape. Cépage translates as grape variety.

Bottled at the estate.

A country wine from the département of the Hérault. This level of wine is only considered to be a superior table wine, therefore the label must also say table wine of France.

appellation **Côtes du Roussillon** and **Côtes du Roussillon Villages** which covers a large part of the département of the Pyrénées-Orientales. Côtes du Roussillon is beginning to rise above the adverse reputation of the Midi with a growing number of serious producers working to improve the quality of their wine. Côtes du Roussillon Villages covers a smaller area including two villages whose names may appear on the label, **Latour de France** and

**Caramany**. The term Villages implies a better wine than the basic appellation. In this instance the quality of the wine justifies the inference. The flavours are redolent of the warm south, as are those of the nearby appellation of **Fitou**. While Côtes du Roussillon can be white, the Villages version and Fitou are only ever red.

The twin appellations of **Minervois** and **Corbières** were promoted from VDQS with the 1985 vintage. Here there are growers who show just what can be done when wine is kept in small barrels for a few months. They have also planted some improving Syrah and Mourvèdre vines to enliven the traditional Midi blend of Carignan, Cinsaut and Grenache. Both are much more important for red than either white or pink wine, and make warm fruity wines with the flavours of the south.

The vineyards between Narbonne and Montpellier are covered by the umbrella appellation of the **Coteaux du Languedoc**, which has several individual crus of which the most important are **St-Chinian**, **La Clape** and **Faugères**. Both the appellation and cru will be on the label. Again red wine features much more than white, the potential for improvement is enormous. There are also some particularly successful vins de pays, often with unorthodox grape varieties such as Cabernet Sauvignon and Chenin Blanc, demonstrating just what can be done with modern equipment to cool fermentation temperatures, or new barrels to mature the wine. Vins de pays are sometimes labelled as vin de cépage, meaning that they come from a single grape variety.

The principal wine of the Gard is the **Costières du Gard**, another new appellation soon to be renamed Costières de Nîmes. Here the wines are lighter than the Coteaux du Languedoc with an immediate fruity impact, a perfumed pepperiness, which makes them more suitable for summer than winter drinking.

# PROVENCE

*I*f you have ever taken a holiday in Provence, eaten bouillabaise in Marseille and sipped wine at a seafront café in St. Tropez, the chances are that you drank a pink **Côtes de Provence** in a peculiar amphora shaped bottle. Provence is better known for pink wines that fit the image of sun, sea and holidays, than reds which offer much more drinking interest. Pink Côtes de Provence is fresh and fruity when young, while red Côtes de Provence has some weight and stature. A group of twenty odd estates are allowed to use the term cru classé, a status of no significance today.

**Coteaux d'Aix-en-Provence** is more seriously red than pink and, like Côtes de Provence, produces a small amount of white wine too. It comes from vineyards covering a large area around the town. When it comes from the subdivision of **Les Baux** or **Coteaux-des-Baux**, then both appellation and sub-division should appear on the label.

In addition there are several smaller appellations of which the most interesting is **Bandol.**

Mourvèdre is the principal grape variety here for the red wine and, blended with other southern varieties, makes fullbodied meaty wines for a cold winter's evening. This is one of the underrated wines of the region. White and pink are made too, but are of much less importance. **Palette** is concentrated in one small but fine estate, Château Simone, while **Cassis** is best known for solid white wines. **Bellet** is a tiny appellation caught up in the suburbs of Nice. A newer appellation is the **Côtes du Lubéron**, while the **Coteaux Varois** has recently been promoted from a vin de pays. The first covers all three colours, and the second red and pink wine. Although Provence may be better known for its pink wine, there is no doubt that the more exciting flavours and better value wines are to be found amongst her reds.

### Bandol

*A simple line drawing conveying an impression of the warm south, with cypress trees.*

*The appellation is Bandol, one of the best of Provence, especially for meaty red wine.*

*Name of the estate. Mas is an old Provençal word for a farmhouse.*

*This wine won a silver medal at the Paris agricultural fair in 1983, considered to be one of the more serious wine awards.*

**BANDOL**
APPELLATION BANDOL CONTRÔLÉE

**MAS de la ROUVIÈRE**

1981

BUNAN VIGNERON AU CASTELLET VAR
MIS EN BOUTEILLE A LA PROPRIETE
FRANCE                    vol net 75cl

*Name of the producer, who is a winemaker in the village of Castellet, in the département of the Var.*

*Bottled at the property.*

# CORSICA

*C*orsica is but a short flight away from Nice, but her wines still retain an individuality consistent with her island heritage. There are three appellations, **Patrimonio**, **Ajaccio** and **Vin de Corse**, which have five crus, namely Sartène, Figari, Porto-Vecchio, Cap Corse and Calvi. In addition there is the picturesque **Vin de Pays de l'Ile de Beauté**. The best wines come from unique and individual Corsican varieties such as Nielluccio and Sciacarello for red wines, which produce flavours reminiscent of the *maquis*, the shrubland which covers much of the interior of the island. Vermentino is the principal white grape which gives dry, fragrant, slightly bitter wines.

### *Vin de Corse*

*A very simple label with a rustic Corsican vineyard scene, and the black Moor's head which features in the island's traditions.*

*Name of the estate.*

*The appellation is Vin de Corse, without any mention of a cru.*

*The producer is A. Nicolaï, who is the owner and producer, at the*

*town of Sartène, with the postal code.*

*Bottled at the property.*

# ALSACE

$A$lsace provides the transition between France and Germany and yet its wines belong to neither country. An historical reason accounts for this diversity for Alsace was German between 1870 and 1919.

You find grape varieties that are not grown anywhere else in France and the names of both producers and vineyards often have a Germanic ring, as do the wine villages. Most Alsace wines are white, but neither sweet like many German wines, nor bone dry or acidic like most French whites, but with a distinctive tangy grapiness of their own.

The basic appellation of the region is **Alsace**, which is usually qualified by the grape variety, the name of which is often the dominant word on the label and determines the taste of the wine.

The simplest of these are Pinot Blanc and Sylvaner, both of which provide elementary quaffing wines. Muscat d'Alsace has a young grapey flavour, while Pinot Gris, which is also known as Tokay d'Alsace, is fuller bodied with some spicy overtones. Both names must be on the label as the EEC has been trying to persuade producers to give up the traditional term Tokay.

Gewürztraminer is the most typical Alsace grape variety, not grown anywhere else in France. It makes distinctive spicy wines that are packed with flavour which you either like or hate. Riesling, again not to be found anywhere else in France, is the region's most distinctive grape, making stylish, elegant wines, especially with some bottle age. A little Pinot Noir is also produced to make a light red wine, with delicate raspberry fruit. Finally Edelzwicker is a blend of grape varieties, usually

Pinot Blanc, Silvaner and sometimes Chasselas.

A recent addition is the appellation of **Alsace grand cru**. These are designated vineyards, that may only be planted with Muscat, Pinot Gris, Riesling or Gewürztraminer and are generally considered to be the best sites in a village. However, the plethora of names, with forty-eight grands crus and more to come, might only confuse the consumer. So some producers prefer to retain their own fantasy names to designate their better wines, such as Trimbach's Riesling Frédéric Emile.

Finally there is **Crémant d'Alsace**, a champagne method sparkling wine that has developed considerably over the last few years.

*Alsace*

*The three prominent things on this label are the appellation, the grape variety and the producer's name.*

*Name of the grape variety.*

*Schlossberg — the name of the vineyard.*

*Schlossberg is a grand cru vineyard, and the wine is therefore of better quality than basic Alsace.*

ALSACE GRAND CRU

**Riesling Schlossberg**

APPELLATION ALSACE GRAND CRU CONTRÔLÉE

**BLANCK** 0.70 l

**Domaine des Comtes de Lupfen**

Mise en Bouteilles au Domaine des Comtes de Lupfen.
Propriété de Paul Blanck et ses fils à Kientzheim (Kaysersberg)
Haut-Rhin - France

*Name of the producer in very prominent letters. He owns the former estate of the Comtes de Lupfen.*

*Bottled at the estate.*

*Property of Paul Blanck and his sons with their address.*

# GERMANY

*T*he key to the quality of German wines is sweetness. The sugar in the grapes determines the quality level of the wine, which is clearly defined in German wine law. The more sugar, the sweeter and better the wine.

There are four broad divisions, **Deutscher Tafelwein**, or German table wine, **Landwein**, which translates literally as 'country wine'; **Qualitätswein bestimmter Anbaugebiet** or a quality wine from a specified region, commonly known as QbA; and finally **Qualitätswein mit Prädikat**, or a quality wine with a Prädikat. The different Prädikat, in ascending order of sweetness and determined by the Oechsle level, or sugar reading, of the grapes, are **Kabinett**, **Spätlese**, **Auslese**, **Beerenauslese** and **Trockenbeerenauslese**. Spätlese means late picked, a wine of a late harvest, while Auslese implies a selection of grapes, usually affected by noble rot and Beerenauslese is a selection of berries. Trocken describes dried berries, that are almost raisinlike.

In addition there is **Eiswein**, literally 'ice wine', made from grapes that have been left on the vines until the middle of winter to be picked and pressed when the juice is frozen. Consequently a significant amount of the water content in the grapes is eliminated. The resulting wine is very sweet and concentrated, almost to the extent of being unbalanced. The sugar reading of the grapes must be the minimum for a Beerenauslese.

As Landwein is considered to be of lesser quality, it can never be sweet, but only trocken or halbtrocken, dry or half-dry, limited to 4 grams of residual sugar per litre for trocken and 18 grams for halbtrocken.

Vintages vary enormously in Germany and Beerenauselese and Trockenbeerenauslese wines are only made in very exceptional years, like 1988. In a dull year, like 1984, there will be few Kabinett wines, let alone Spätlese or Auslese.

There is a logic too, about the geographical organization of German wines. Deutscher Tafelwein can come from four broad areas, namely **Rhein–Mosel**, **Bayern**, **Neckar** and **Oberrhein**, which are in turn divided up into fifteen Landwein districts and eleven Anbaugebiete for quality wine. The Anbaugebiete encompass thirty-five Bereiche, or districts, which in turn contain 152 Grosslagen or groups of vineyards, which divide into about 2,600 Einzellagen or single named vineyards.

There is a similar logic in the organization of the label. The first word of the name is the village, the second the vineyard site. Third comes the grape variety and fourth the Prädikat. All German wine labels must carry an AP or Amtliche Prüfungsnummer to show that the wines have undergone tasting and analytical tests. The AP. number on the label below is made up as follows:

A.P. No. 4920 001 007 88
4 – the examination board number.
920 – the number of the commune where the wine was bottled.
001 – the bottler's registered number.

### Blue Nun

*The emphasis is on the name of the brand, the most eye-catching part of the label.*

*The German company in Mainz who produce the wine.*

*Shipped and bottled by the London company of H. Sichel & Sons Ltd, with their London postal code.*

*A quality wine–Liebfraumilch from the Rheinhessen.*

*Volume, contents, country of origin.*

*The AP number to show that the wine has undergone the obligatory tasting and analysis. See text for explanation of how the number is composed.*

007 – the bottler's application number; in other words this is the seventh bottling of Blue Nun in the year.

88 – the year of application for bottling.

The problem is that so many German wine names are often unpronounceable, further confusion being caused by the illegible gothic script. It is no wonder that Liebfraumilch with easy names like Blue Nun and Black Tower has become so popular on the export market. Liebfraumilch is a QbA wine that comes from either the **Rheinhessen, Rheinpfalz** or **Nahe**. It takes its name from the vineyard of the Liebfrauenkirche in the suburbs of Worms. At its best it is an easy-to-drink, fruity, slightly sweet white wine and a wonderful introduction to the finer wines of Germany.

German wine is above all white. A tiny amount of red wine is produced in the **Ahr** and also in **Baden**, for which Spätburgunder (the German name for Pinot Noir) is the usual grape variety. The same criteria of sweetness can also apply to these red wines.

It is Riesling that makes the best white wines of Germany. This is a grape variety that survives cold winters and, in the right climatic conditions, develops noble rot, to make delicately sweet, honeyed wines, low in alcohol and delicious to drink on their own. In those years when vineyards have no noble rot, the process of adding *süssreserve*, or sweet reserve, is permitted up to and including Auslese quality. *Süssreserve* is unfermented grape juice which is added to the fermented wine to give extra sweetness. It must be of the same Prädikat quality.

The essential problem with German wines is that they do not go well with food, although they are perfect to drink before or after a meal. However, this apparent handicap has led German winemakers to experiment with drier wines more suited to accompany a meal. The new trocken and halbtrocken wines are designed to fill this gap. Although a

## Hochheim

*An example of the best, or depending on your point of view, worst of German excesses in labelling. Queen Victoria stopped to watch the vintage at a vineyard in Hochheim which was subsequently renamed after her. The label carries the royal coat of arms and depicts the monument erected at the vineyard to commemorate the queen's visit.*

Hochheim is the name of the village; 'er' added to the name turns it into an adjective.

Grape variety.

Name of the vineyard.

The region.

The Prädikat, qualified by the words Qualitätswein mit Prädikat and the AP number.

Estate bottled by GM Pabstmann Nachf. – the successors of the Pabstmann family, who owned the vineyard at the time of the queen's visit. Nachf. is an abbreviation for Nachfolger.

## *Johannisberg*

*The opposite extreme, an example of elegant clarity and legibility. The German wine shippers, Deinhard & Co. are attempting to simplify their German labels and have produced a series of wines, labelled only by village. Illustrated with the family crest; the company is nearly 200 years old.*

*What the label does not tell you is the grape variety– which is Riesling– nor the degree of sweetness–which is off dry. Without a vineyard name it can be assumed that it is a blend of wines from vineyards within the village of Johannisberg. In buying this wine, you are placing your confidence in Deinhard's expertise as German wine producers.*

*Johannisberg is one of the best villages of the Rheingau.*

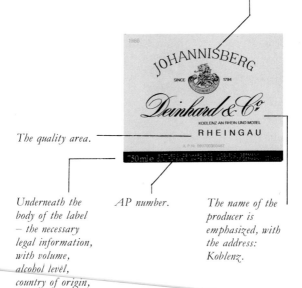

*The quality area.*

*Underneath the body of the label – the necessary legal information, with volume, alcohol level, country of origin, and quality category.*

*AP number.*

*The name of the producer is emphasized, with the address: Koblenz.*

Landwein must be trocken or halbtrocken, it is also possible to have a trocken or halbtrocken Prädikat, in which the sugar in the grapes has been completely fermented, with no addition of *süssreserve*. So far many of the new wave of trocken wines lack the intrinsic quality of German wines and taste rather skeletal, with the possible exception of those from Baden and the Palatinate (Rheinpfalz).

The most popular grape variety is Müller–Thurgau, which is responsible for an enormous amount of cheap and cheerful quaffing wine from the Mosel, and also for Liebfraumilch. Silvaner used to be widely grown, but is decreasing except in **Franconia** where it makes attractive grassy wines. Then there are several new crossings, such as Kerner, Huxelrebe, Reichensteiner, etc., designed to combat the harsh climate to produce sugar-packed grapes.

The finest German wines come from the quality regions of the Rhine and the Mosel. The **Mosel–Saar–Ruwer**, to give its full name, makes deliciously steely, flowery white wines, with a delicate fragrance. The wines of the Rhine, which in England are traditionally known as hock, from the village of Hochheim, are a little fuller and richer. They are at their most elegant in the **Rheingau**, while the wines of the Nahe are a cross between those of the Mosel and the Rheingau. In the Rheinhessen the wines become a little fuller, and in the Rheinpfalz to the south, even heavier. The **Ahr**, a tributary of the Mittelrhein, is best known for its red wine. The wines from the **Mittelrhein**, **Württemberg** and the **Hessischer Bergstrasse** are rarely seen abroad. Baden, the region closest to Alsace, makes some of the most full-flavoured dry wines in the country. Franconia is known for its drier wines in their distinctive squat dumpy bottles. The essence of German wine lies with a flowery Mosel or a honeyed Rhine wine from a reputable estate in a good vintage.

# AUSTRIA

$\mathcal{T}$here are close similarities between Austrian and German wines in that they have the same system of Prädikat, with its recognition of sweetness as a quality factor. Again the scale goes from Tafelwein to Trockenbeerenauslese, but Austria recognizes an additional category, Ausbruch, which comes between Beerenauselese and Trockenbeerenauslese. A Kabinett wine is not considered to be a Prädikat wine.

The important difference between Germany and Austria is that the latter enjoys a much warmer continental climate so her grapes ripen more readily and the wines are fuller and richer. Consequently, *süssreserve* is not allowed in Austrian Prädikat wines. Red wine is more important too, with grapes such as Blaufrankisch and Zweigelt. As in Germany, Riesling makes some stylish wines with nobly rotten grapes. Grüner Veltliner is the other distinctive Austrian grape variety, making drier, rather smoky white wines. Welschriesling is important too.

The vineyards of Austria are concentrated in the eastern half of the country, in the regions of **Burgenland**, **Niederösterreich** and **Steiermark**, which are in turn divided into smaller areas, the names of which feature on the label, as does the Prädikat and the grape variety.

Austrian wines suffered a great disservice at the hands of the perpetrators of her wine scandal, and her wines merit far greater attention. They are well made and offer good value for money with consistent quality.

### *Wachau*

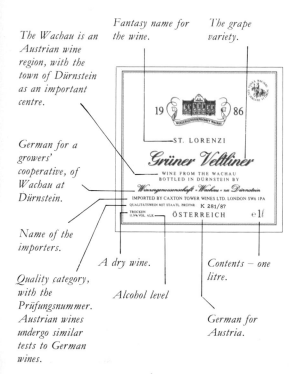

*Fantasy name for the wine.*

*The grape variety.*

*The Wachau is an Austrian wine region, with the town of Dürnstein as an important centre.*

*German for a growers' cooperative, of Wachau at Dürnstein.*

*Name of the importers.*

*Quality category, with the Prüfungsnummer. Austrian wines undergo similar tests to German wines.*

*A dry wine.*

*Alcohol level*

*Contents – one litre.*

*German for Austria.*

# ITALY

*I*taly is a country of contradictions and surprises. She has a wine law modelled on the French system, but whereas in France, with perhaps one or two exceptions, it can be assumed that all the country's fine wines have an appellation, in Italy it is by no means the case that all her good wines have official recognition. The principal category of Italian wine is Denominazione di Origine Controlata, DOC for short. The foundations of the system were laid in 1963 and there are now some 230 odd wines which have been given this distinction. They are scattered all over the country, but the greatest concentration is in the vineyards of the north, of Piedmont, the Veneto and Tuscany.

DOC lays down standards, delimiting the vine-yards, defining the grape varieties, limiting yields, determining the type of wine, methods of cultivation and vinification procedures. Unfortunately DOC has been granted not only to well-established wines with a reputation, but also to obscure and undeserving ones where the standards are not always rigorously applied. There are numerous DOCs which are of little importance outside their own region. One might be forgiven for wondering why they were ever given that status in the first place.

A superior category has also been instituted, Denominazione di Origine Controlata e Garantita (DOCG), with even stricter regulations. These wines are submitted to strict analysis and tasting tests, and quality is controlled more rigorously than for DOC. So far six wines have been given this distinction. The first four were **Barolo** and **Barbaresco** from Peidmont, and **Brunello di Montalcino** and **Vino Nobile di Montepulciano** from Tuscany. Nobody seriously disputes the valid-ity of this distinction as these wines are generally considered to be the best in their areas. Next comes **Chianti**, not just the better areas of **Chianti Classico**, **Rufina** and **Colli Fiorentini**, but the whole mass of this wine, with its wide variation of quality. However, it seems that DOCG has had some effect upon improving the overall quality of Chianti, but it is arguable that DOCG for the whole area is inappropriate. More open to criticism is the granting of DOCG to **Albana di Romagna**, an insignificant dry white wine, with an unmemorable taste, which rarely travels outside Emilia Romagna. This has thrown the whole concept of DOCG into disrepute. It seems that political clout is more important than vinous quality.

Perhaps then it is no surprise that some of the best wines of Italy are neither DOC nor DOCG. Italians are individualists and hate to conform. Conse-

### Chianti

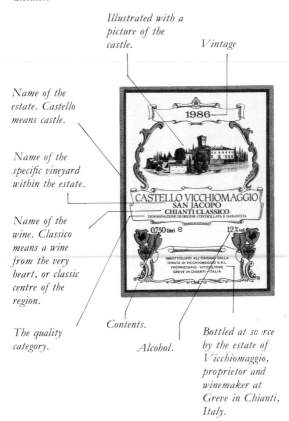

Illustrated with a picture of the castle.

Vintage

Name of the estate. Castello means castle.

Name of the specific vineyard within the estate.

Name of the wine. Classico means a wine from the very heart, or classic centre of the region.

The quality category.

Contents.

Alcohol.

Bottled at source by the estate of Vicchiomaggio, proprietor and winemaker at Greve in Chianti, Italy.

quently, although vino da tavola on the label implies a wine of lesser quality, it may in fact be of infinitely superior quality to a DOC or DOCG. There is really no way of knowing this for certain unless you are familiar with the producer, but the presentation of the bottle and label provides a clue, as will the price. If the vino da tavola is more expensive than the corresponding DOC, the producer certainly considers it to be the better wine and he will have lavished more care and attention upon it.

## *Valpolicella*

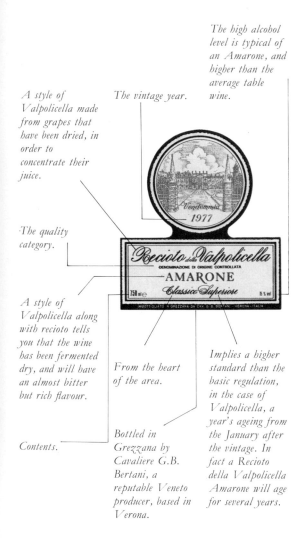

The high alcohol level is typical of an Amarone, and higher than the average table wine.

The vintage year.

A style of Valpolicella made from grapes that have been dried, in order to concentrate their juice.

The quality category.

A style of Valpolicella along with recioto tells you that the wine has been fermented dry, and will have an almost bitter but rich flavour.

Contents.

From the heart of the area.

Bottled in Grezzana by Cavaliere G.B. Bertani, a reputable Veneto producer, based in Verona.

Implies a higher standard than the basic regulation, in the case of Valpolicella, a year's ageing from the January after the vintage. In fact a Recioto della Valpolicella Amarone will age for several years.

The very basic quality of vino da tavola, without any indication of provenance can be dismissed, being of no more interest than basic French vin de table. It is the next category, the vino da tavola con indicazione geografica, or vino tipico, which equates to vin de pays in France, and which includes some of the most exciting experimental wines, made from grape varieties not allowed within the corresponding DOCs of their region.

What follows is a brief sketch of the main regions, describing what comes from where, working south region by region, and paying, as always, attention to what is actually on the label. The region of Piedmont in northwest Italy produces what are arguably some of Italy's finest wines, namely Barolo and Barbaresco. Both are reds of considerable stature, wines of great concentration made from the Nebbiolo grape. These are wines aged in wood and then in bottle for several years before they are ready to drink. There are other lighter variations of the Nebbiolo grape, and these usually feature on the label. Other grape varieties are also mentioned in several, mainly red, DOCs, of which Barbera and Dolcetto are the most important. Both are lighter than Nebbiolo, and Dolcetto, as the name implies, has an element of sweetness, with some fresh acidity, making a wine for early drinking. A name like **Dolcetto d'Alba**, means a wine from the Dolcetto grape produced in the province of Alba. Vineyard names sometimes feature on the label, occasionally preceded by the word *vigna*, meaning vineyard, or by the word *bricco*, which is a Piedmontese word for a hilltop, considered to be the superior site.

The best known wines of northeast Italy are the white **Soave** and the red **Bardolino** and **Valpolicella**. Bardolino takes its name from the lakeside village on Lake Garda and is light and fruity, while Valpolicella can be a more serious wine, especially if it is a **Recioto Amarone**, which means that it has been made from grapes dried until well into the winter and then fermented until no sugar is left in the juice. The result is a rich concentrated raisiny wine of immense flavour. Good Soave is dry and nutty, while bad Soave is bland and boring, and occasionally it may be sparkling.

North of Lake Garda are the vineyards of Trentino and the Alto Adige. The DOC of **Trentino** covers several different grape varieties, which appear on the label and indicate the style of wine. The best is Cabernet, which may be either Cabernet Sauvignon or Cabernet Franc, or a blend of both and makes a full, fruity red wine.

Further north in the Alto Adige or Südtirol the grape variety is nearly always part of the name of the wine on the label. There are some attractive dry whites from Chardonnay, various Muscats, Pinot Bianco, and so on. Historical reasons necessitate the presence of both German and Italian terminology, making for truly bilingual wine labels.

Towards the Yugoslav border are the wines of the province of Friuli–Venezia–Giulia. DOCs such as **Collio** and **Colli Orientali del Friuli** are based on single grape varieties which again always feature on the label as part of the wine name. The whites are nearly all dry, with the exception of **Piccolit** an overpriced sweet wine, and the reds from Cabernet, Merlot and Refosco are soft and fruity.

Central Italy covers the provinces of Emilia Romagna, Tuscany, Umbria, Lazio and the Marches. Some of Italy's most exciting wine making comes from Tuscany. Brunello di Montalcino deserves its status of DOCG for this is one of the great red wines of Italy, made from the Brunello or Sangiovese grape grown in vineyards around the town of Montalcino, and aged in wood for a minimum of four years. The new DOC **Rosso di Montalcino**, from the same vineyards, but with a shorter ageing requirement, offers a lighter and similar taste at a more affordable price.

Vino Nobile di Montepulciano is nothing more

than a superior Chianti, but the best is very fine. **Rossi di Montepulciano** is the parallel DOC. **Carmignano**, a red DOC close to Florence, offers serious red wine, including a small amount of Cabernet Sauvignon. **Vernaccia di San Gimignano** is a dry, nutty white wine. Most popular of all is Chianti covering a large area of Tuscany, with seven sub-zones; **Classico**, **Colli Fiorentini**, **Rufina**, **Colli Aretini**, **Colline Pisane**, **Montaleano** and **Colli Senese**. However, the wave of experimentation in Tuscany was born of the faded reputation of Chianti and the need to improve the white wines of the region. Growers who felt there was more to life than indifferent Chianti have

### Vino da Tavola

*An elegant label for a distinguished wine, the forerunner of the many excellent Italian table wines that do not conform to DOC regulations.*

*The appearance of this label will tell you that the wine is no ordinary table wine.*

*Vintage.*

*Name of the wine and also the geographical identity of the table wine – as in Vino da tavola di Sassicaia.*

**SASSICAIA**

**1984**

TENUTA SAN GUIDO

Imbottigliato all'origine dal produttore
Tenuta San Guido - Bolgheri (107 Lt)

VINO DA TAVOLA DI SASSICAIA

750 ml e          ITALIA          12,5% vol.

*Name of the estate.*

*Bottled at source by the producer at Tenuta San Guido, at Bolgheri, with the postal code.*

*Contents, country, alcohol.*

### Orvieto

Name of the wine.

From the heart of the production area.

Quality category.

Dry; Orvieto can also be slightly sweet or abboccato.

As well as owning vineyards, Antinori are also merchants, buying grapes and wine for blending. There is no mention on this label that they are producers of this wine, only bottlers.

Bottled at San Casciano; VP is short for Val di Pesa, with the postal code, by the Marchesi L & P Antinori. SpA – a limited company, based in Florence.

Name of the producer, given almost as much prominence as the wine name. Antinori are one of the best in Tuscany.

begun to experiment with grape varieties not commonly found in Tuscany. The first of these wines was Sassicaia, made from Cabernet Sauvignon and Cabernet Franc. This set the example and others followed, first Antinori with Tignanello made from Sangiovese blended with Cabernet Sauvignon. Now almost every serious grower has his *vino alternativo*, which may be a blend of Cabernet and Sangiovese or a wine made from one or the other. It is usually aged in small oak barrels.

It is not only red wine that has been the subject of such experimentation. Chardonnay and Sauvignon have been planted too, to enliven the dull dry whites made from the common Tuscan varieties of Trebbiano and Malvasia. Each of these super wines has its own fantasy name, and even the most ardent lover of Tuscan wine has some trouble in identifying the exact contents of such wines as Cepparello and Flaccinello. A glossary is needed to decipher some of the names.

The adjoining province of Emilia Romagna is best known for **Lambrusco**, a lightly sparkling, often slightly sweet, white or pink wine which is made for the export market; the Italians drink it red and dry. The other surrounding provinces of Tuscany are better known for their white wines. Umbria is the home of **Orvieto**, which can be secco, dry, or abboccato, slightly sweet. The Lungarotti family are making some exciting wines under the DOC **Torgiano** label from Cabernet Sauvignon and Chardonnay, as well as traditional grape varieties. The Marches make **Verdicchio dei Castelli di Jesi**, which is firmly dry, while Lazio is the home of **Frascati**, the dry white wine the Romans drink.

The further south you travel, the more scattered are the parcels of quality wines. The DOCs or interesting vini da tavola are fewer and further apart in the toe and heel of Italy. Dry white **Greco di Tufo** and **Fiano di Avellino** and the full-flavoured red **Taurasi** are unusual. **Aglianico del Vulture** is full bodied and richly red while **Montepulciano di Abruzzo** makes warm fruity reds. In this instance Montepulciano is the grape variety and has nothing to do with Vino Nobile.

The island of Sicily is best known for its dessert wine, **Marsala**, but there are some good table wines too. Best known of all is Corvo, a brand name for some sound red and white wine. Regaleali is another vino da tavola to look out.

Sardinia is more isolated than Sicily, so its wines tend to bypass mainstream Italian viticulture. **Canonau di Sardegna** is the most common red wine, with flavours varying from sweet to dry.

# SPAIN

$T$hink of Spain and **Rioja** is the first wine name (apart from sherry) which comes to mind. However, the wines of Spain are so much more than that. The Spanish wine industry has undergone an enormous transition over the last ten or fifteen years, with vast improvements in vinification methods and techniques. The country now offers immensely good-value drinking with some interesting flavours.

A system of Denominación de Origen (DO) has been developed, covering the country's main wine areas. This lays down the grape varieties for each wine, but without determining the precise style of wine made, so that the variation of taste within each can be considerable. A Rioja, for example, may be red, white or pink. The white in particular allows for a whole range of tastes from sweet to dry, oak-aged to young and fresh.

A Consejo Regulador, or regulating body, for each DO guarantees the authenticity of the wine, with its stamp on the label. A more exacting category is also envisaged: Denominación de Origen Calificada (DOCa). As yet no wine has been given this status.

A lengthy maturation in oak has always been an intrinsic part of Spanish wine making, so the terms reserva and gran reserva often feature on a Spanish wine label. These wines are only made in the very best years, when the quality of the wines warrants extended ageing. Reservas are given a minimum of three years ageing for red, and two years for white

### *Rioja*

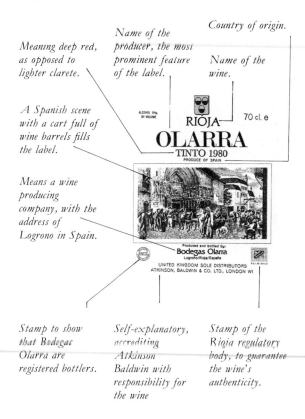

Country of origin.

Name of the producer, the most prominent feature of the label.

Name of the wine.

*Meaning deep red, as opposed to lighter clarete.*

*A Spanish scene with a cart full of wine barrels fills the label.*

*Means a wine producing company, with the address of Logrono in Spain.*

*Stamp to show that Bodegas Olarra are registered bottlers.*

*Self-explanatory, accrediting Atkinson Baldwin with responsibility for the wine*

*Stamp of the Rioja regulatory body, to guarantee the wine's authenticity.*

## Penedés

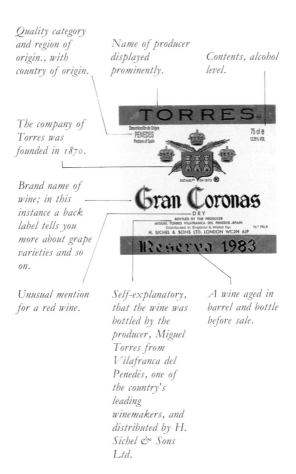

Quality category and region of origin., with country of origin.

Name of producer displayed prominently.

Contents, alcohol level.

The company of Torres was founded in 1870.

Brand name of wine; in this instance a back label tells you more about grape varieties and so on.

Unusual mention for a red wine.

Self-explanatory, that the wine was bottled by the producer, Miguel Torres from Vilafranca del Penedés, one of the country's leading winemakers, and distributed by H. Sichel & Sons Ltd.

A wine aged in barrel and bottle before sale.

and pink wines, of which one year is spent in oak for reds, and six months for whites and pinks. Gran Reserva reds require two years ageing in oak and three in bottle or vice versa, while whites and pinks have four years ageing, of which six months must be in oak. Another common term is crianza, which means that a red wine has been aged for a minimum of one year in wood and a white or pink six months. Sin crianza indicates no wood ageing at all.

**Rioja** sets the benchmark for many Spanish wines. The flavours are dominated by the maturation in American oak barrels, which gives the wines a distinctive sweet vanilla flavour, with a firm dry finish. Whites are sometimes aged in this way, but the modern trend has been towards cool fermentation sin crianza wines, which are full and fruity, but sometimes lacking in regional definition.

More interesting white wines come from **Penedés** where the pioneering winemaker Miguel Torres has experimented with innovatory grape varieties, such as Chardonnay and Gewürztraminer, not to mention Cabernet Sauvignon for his red wines. In northern Spain the traditional white grape varieties are Parellada, Xarel-lo and Macabeo, none of which has a very distinctive flavour making dry, rather solid wines, that benefit either from some oak ageing, or from the injection of a dollop of something more exciting, such as Chardonnay, to give more flavour. As will be seen later acceptable sparkling wine is also made. Red wines are dominated by Garnacha and Tempranillo.

Further south the wines are headier and more alcoholic. The sunbaked vineyards of **Valencia**, **Alicante** and **Jumilla** produce warm, rich red wines, that demand to be drunk with food. The Spanish plain of **La Mancha** used to symbolize the worst of Spanish wine making, with earthy oxidized whites made from Airen, and overcooked reds from Monastrell. Now, however, modern vinification methods have made their impact and the quality of the wine has improved dramatically.

Spain is a wine country of untapped potential. With her recent entry to the Common Market, her wines are assuming greater importance and there are undiscovered treasures from some of the newer DOs. Wines from **Ribera del Duero**, **Somontano**, **Toro** and **Navarra** provide some warm fuity reds, while the white wines of **Rueda** and **Ribeiro** offer dry fragrant flavours.

# PORTUGAL

*P*ort, **Madeira** and Mateus Rosé are the catchword names of Portugal, but like Spain, it is a country of untapped drinking potential, with undiscovered delights waiting to be found. Again, like Spain, vinification methods have improved enormously in recent years. Ageing in wood is a vital part of Portuguese wine making, and was often overdone, but now happily, the trend is towards red wines with real fruit and whites with attractive fresh acidity.

Portugal has a system of appellations, called Regiao Demarcada, and in addition a handful of areas are recognized as Vinho Regiao, because they are hoping for recognition as demarcated regions. A seal of origin guarantees the authenticity of the demarcated wines. The terms velha, reserva and garrafeira are often found on Portuguese wine labels and are now legally defined. Reserva is a vintage wine, with half a degree more alcohol than the minimum requirement, but no ageing requirement. Garrafeira, on the other hand, demands, as well as the extra half degree of alcohol, a minimum of three years ageing including one in bottle, for red wines, and for white, one year's ageing, including six months in bottle. Generally the producer sells his best wines as a garrafeira, upon which he hangs his reputation. A garrafeira may be a blend of wine from several areas or vineyards, provided there is no mention of a regiao demarcada on the label.

Velha, meaning old, is another common term and must now apply to wines with a minimum age of three years for reds and two years for whites.

The most exciting red table wines of Portugal come from **Bairrada**. We had hardly heard of this area five years ago, but now it is at the heart of the considerable improvement in Portuguese wines. There are some distinctive full-bodied reds with tannin and spicy, warm fruity flavours.

**Dão** is another important red, traditionally with a rather dry, austere and unappealing flavour. Again, things are changing so that fruit is all important. As with Bairrada, Dão is a serious wine to be drunk with food, although the whites are unimportant.

The best white wine comes from the Minho region of northern Portugal, where **Vinho Verde** is made. Although red is also made, only the white is exported. It is low in alcohol, and usually with a hint of a carbon dioxide prickle, making a fresh, fragrant and dry wine for summer drinking.

**Bucelas**, **Colares** and **Carcavelos** are traditional names that rarely travel. Look instead for table wines from the **Douro**, flavoursome reds with a hint of the liquorice found in port. The **Alentejo** is as yet only a Vinho Regiao. It covers a large part of Portugal north of the Algarve and is an area about which we shall hear more, for fine red wines. The

### *Dão*

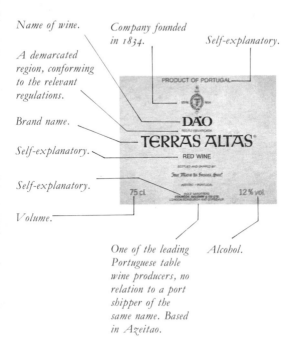

*Name of wine.*

*Company founded in 1834.*

*Self-explanatory.*

*A demarcated region, conforming to the relevant regulations.*

*Brand name.*

*Self-explanatory.*

*Self-explanatory.*

*Volume.*

*One of the leading Portuguese table wine producers, no relation to a port shipper of the same name. Based in Azeitao.*

*Alcohol.*

**Ribatejo**, a Vinho Regiao, northeast of Lisbon is another area of great potential.

Some of Portugal's best table wines do not conform to any appellation. The company of J.M. da Fonseca, whose wines are readily available abroad, produces wines such as **Periquita**, **Pasmados**, and **Camarate**, from the Estemadura, north of Lisbon. These have a quality which is superior when compared to the region's other wines. Quinta de Bacalhoa is another example of what can be achieved with imaginative modern wine making. These are indicative of the direction that Portuguese wines are taking. The good ones offer tremendous value; the bad are still very bad and can only improve.

# THE
# MEDITERRANEAN

## LEBANON

*T*he wines of the Lebanon are represented abroad
by one estate – Château Musar in the Bekàa valley.
The label is self-explanatory, giving prominence to
the estate name and its owner, Serge Hochar, who
courageously keeps this vineyard going against all
odds in war-ridden Lebanon. There is no mention of
grape varieties, but they are, in fact, Cabernet
Sauvignon, Syrah and Cinsaut.

## GREECE

*F*or most people Greek wine is epitomized by well
chilled Retsina drunk on a sunsoaked holiday, or
maybe a Muscat from the island of Samos, or a
branded table wine such as Demestica. In fact, a

system of regional appellations is being developed, of which there were twenty-six at the last count, such as red, white and pink **Côtes de Meliton** and fullbodied red **Naoussa** and **Nemea**. Old-fashioned production methods need to be modernized before Greek wines can make more of an impact abroad. Greek labels tend to be an exotic mixture of the Greek and French languages, in Greek and Roman script.

### *Côtes de Meliton*

*Greek wine labels tend to be bilingual, with French translations of the Greek.*

*Name of the estate, one of the leading producers of Greece.*

*Produce of Greece.*

*An area of origin, qualified by an appellation.*

*Bottled at the château.*

*Volume.*

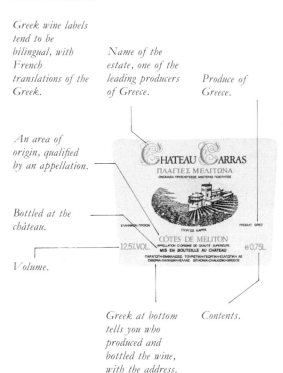

*Greek at bottom tells you who produced and bottled the wine, with the address.*

*Contents.*

# EASTERN EUROPE

# YUGOSLAVIA

Yugoslavia is best known for Lutomer Laski Rizling, an innocuous white wine, made not from the German Riesling but from the less flavoursome Welschriesling. Laski Rizling or Grasevina is the Yugoslav synonym.

Yugoslavia has a system of appellations of origin, covering all the country's vineyards. Above basic table wine level, the label will always give an area of origin, which will be qualified, either by Kvalitetno vino, meaning a quality wine, or Vrhunsko vino, a top quality wine. The distinction between them is the number of marks out of 100 the wine receives when it is presented for tasting—70 as opposed to 85. The wine law also allows for levels of sweetness, the equivalent of the German Prädikat, but these wines are rarely found abroad.

Apart from Laski Rizling, Yugoslavia's wines are a mixture of the traditional, with modern encroachments. There are grape varieties such as Sauvignon, Gewürztraminer and Merlot which are vinified in the modern manner, while the picturesque sounding Tiger's Milk is made from the obscure Ranina or Bouvier grape. More original are the full-bodied red wines such as **Vranac**, **Dingač** and **Postup**, which rarely stray abroad.

### Lutomer

*The grape variety.*

*Lutomer reads like a brand name; in fact this is the area of production, amplified by the Yugoslav name Ljutomersko Ormoske Gorice.*

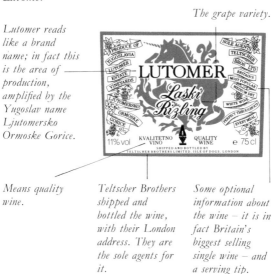

*Means quality wine.*

*Teltscher Brothers shipped and bottled the wine, with their London address. They are the sole agents for it.*

*Some optional information about the wine – it is in fact Britain's biggest selling single wine – and a serving tip.*

# HUNGARY

One of the world's great sweet white wines comes from Hungary, namely **Tokay**, or **Tokaji**, made like Sauternes from nobly rotten grapes. There are various qualities of Tokay, depending on the degree of sweetness. Szamorodni, meaning literally 'as it comes' is more or less dry, while the word Aszu indicates that the wine is sweet. How sweet depends upon the number of *putts* or *puttonyos*, so that three equates to Auslese, four or five to Beerenauselese and six, which is rare, would be approaching a Trockenbeerenauselese. However, there is even a sweeter and rarer Tokay Essence, which is traditionally credited with life-restoring powers.

### *Hungary*

*Produce of Hungary – self-explanatory.*

*Bulls Blood – Prominence given to the name of wine, with Hungarian name underneath.*

*Egribikaver – Hungarian for wine and Minosegi means best quality as opposed to ordinary wine.*

*Egervin – name of the Hungarian producers, a state monopoly. Hedges & Butler shipped it.*

Rather more mundane is **Bull's Blood**, the brand name for a red wine which takes its name from a popular legend about the Magyars defeating the Turks at the battle of Eger in the 16th century. The Magyar warriors sustained their strength with wine, the red stains on their beards being mistaken by the Turks, who drank no wine, for the blood of bulls. Today the wine does not live up to the legend and Egri Bikaver, the Hungarian name for Bull's Blood, is an unpretentious, mild red wine.

Vineyards around Lake Balaton produce medium dry white Welschriesling or Olaszrizling, but otherwise the reputation of Hungarian wine depends upon Tokay.

# BULGARIA

$O$f all the eastern European countries, Bulgaria has adapted her wines most successfully to the taste of the international market. It was only after the Second World War that the Bulgarian government decided to exploit the enormous potential of the country's vineyards and reorganize the industry for export. A considerable investment programme has created vineyards of Chardonnay, Cabernet Sauvignon, and Merlot, while retaining some more individual Bulgarian flavours from grapes like Gamza, Melnik and Mavrud.

A Bulgarian system of appellations has been established, so that broadly speaking there are five main areas, which in turn split into (at the last count) twenty Controliran regions, each for one or more specific grape varieties. In addition there are a growing number of what the Bulgarians call 'wines of declared geographical origin'. Regulations for the Controliran regions are very strictly controlled, in the manner of a French appellation, with a carefully defined vineyard area, limited yields, and so on. A Controliran wine says so on the label and bears an official stamp to that effect. The Controliran regions include names such as **Novi Pazar** for Chardonnay, **Svichtov** for pure Cabernet Sauvignon and **Asenovgrad** for Mavrud. Wines of declared geographical origin are akin to vins de pays, in that they come from an administrative area and just say, for example, **Suhindol** region.

There is also a newly defined quality of reserve wines, which require a minimum period of ageing. A red reserve wine from a declared geographical origin must have spent a minimum of three years in wood, and from a Controliran region four years. For white wine, the time is two and three years, respectively.

Mehana, meaning a bistro or café in Bulgarian, is the popular brand name for basic Bulgarian wine. The better Bulgarian wines also mention a grape variety on the label, in which case the wine is made only from that particular variety. Bulgarian wine making improves year by year. These are certainly wines which offer excellent drinking value with both international and indigenous flavours.

### Bulgaria

*Bulgaria's wine labels portray the successful adaptation of her wines to western European taste.*

*The principal difference between these two labels is that Suhindol is a controliran zone, and Preslav is not.*

*The first label carries an official stamp to that effect, otherwise they both tell you the grape variety, Chardonnay and Gamza, describe the wine as fine and give the name*

*and address of the importers, Bulgarian Vintners.*

# NORTH AMERICA

California is the largest wine producing state in North America, although vines of some description are now grown in nearly all fifty states, from Texas to Missouri, Arkansas to Hawaii.

Mexican missionaries brought viticulture to the Golden State in the 18th century and Europeans founded wineries in the 1850s, many of which were disbanded during Prohibition in the 1920s. The new wave of Californian wine making began in the 1960s when Robert Mondavi opened the first new winery in the Napa Valley since before Prohibition. It was an exciting turning point in the fortunes of the Californian wine industry.

California looks to Europe. The grape varieties are those of the classic areas of France, with Cabernet Sauvignon and Chardonnay making an impact above all. Technology is the most modern, with no expense spared on new oak barrels and the latest equipment, which combined with a refreshingly questioning attitude, makes for exciting wine production.

Vines are grown over most parts of the state, with considerable variations of style and flavour. There is a broad climatic range from cool coastal areas to the sunsoaked central plain which makes jug wine in prolific quantity.

Although Californians have argued against the French attachment to the importance of the soil, the underlying factor of the appellation system, their own new system of appellations, or Authorized Viticultural Areas, the first of which were established in 1980, has given the vineyard areas some definition. Californians still think nothing of buying grapes from two vineyards a couple of hundred miles apart and blending them in a central winery, but this must now be clearly shown on the label. A California Zinfandel may come from grapes grown anywhere in the state, while a **Napa Valley** Sauvignon implies that 75 per cent of the grapes are Sauvignon Blanc from the Napa Valley. With this flexible percentage there is still room for manoeuvre, but some wineries prefer to ignore the Authorized Viticultural Areas, AVAs as they are called.

In all there are nearly sixty AVAs covering most of the state, with defined areas of production, some of which have an established identity, while others have not progressed much further than the statute book. Confusingly, it is not necessary to qualify the name of an AVA with the words Authorized Viticultural Area. Consequently, a vineyard name could be mistaken for an AVA. Nor does an AVA entail any standard of quality, only a guarantee of origin.

There is no doubt that the winery name and the grape variety are still the key factors in the choice a wine. Although the AVA may assume gre importance, especially as grape varieties are be ociated with specific areas, for example **arneros Creek** Chardonnay, e st concentration of winerie

Napa and Sonoma valleys to the north of San Francisco. In Napa there are many of the famous names such as Mondavi, Joseph Phelps, Heitz, Sterling etc., while the **Sonoma Valley** and the **Russian River** have a similar concentration of talent. **Chalk Hill**, **Alexander Valley** and **Dry Creek** are other possible AVAs within Sonoma county.

**Mendocino County** is the most northern vineyard area of California, while to the south of San Francisco, vines stretch in pockets down to the Mexican border. There are numerous AVAs, of which the most exciting include **Chalone**, **Paso Robles** and the **Santa Ynez Valley**.

Zinfandel is the most peculiarly Californian grape variety. It may have its origins in Europe and was probably brought to California by Agoston Haraszthy, who is considered one of the pioneers of

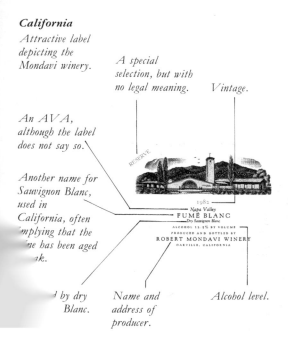

*California*
*Attractive label depicting the Mondavi winery.*

*A special selection, but with no legal meaning.*

*Vintage.*

*An AVA, although the label does not say so.*

*Another name for Sauvignon Blanc, used in California, often implying that the \_ne has been aged \_k.*

*\_d by dry Blanc.*

*Name and address of producer.*

*Alcohol level.*

## *California*

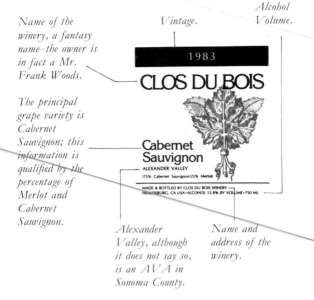

Name of the winery, a fantasy name–the owner is in fact a Mr. Frank Woods.

Vintage.

Alcohol Volume.

The principal grape variety is Cabernet Sauvignon; this information is qualified by the percentage of Merlot and Cabernet Sauvignon.

Alexander Valley, although it does not say so, is an AVA in Sonoma County.

Name and address of the winery.

Californian viticulture. Versatility is the essence of Zinfandel. It makes pale pink wines, nouveau styles, fullbodied, fruity, berry flavoured table wines and heady port styles.

The most outstanding red grape variety is indisputably Cabernet Sauvignon, which is given the same serious treatment as in any Bordeaux château. Californian winemakers discuss the merits of Allier and Limousin oak, and of toasted and steamed barrels, while the Bordelais are taking an interest in California with projects such as Opus One and Dominus, associated with Châteaux Mouton Rothschild and Pétrus, respectively.

The true flavour of Pinot Noir is elusive, which Californians have found hard to capture. The grape variety thrives in a cooler climate and the best California Pinot Noir comes from Carneros Creek.

Chardonnay is the essence of white wine making. It is given the Burgundian treatment of oak ageing

## Long Island

The name of the winery.

The AVA, although it does not say so, on Long Island.

Grape variety.

Vintage.

Implies a special selection of wine from that estate. This information is amplified by the footnote telling you how the wine was made and matured.

Alcohol level.

Sulphur dioxide is used by virtually all winemakers.

Name and address of the winery.

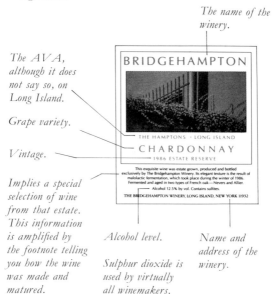

BRIDGEHAMPTON

THE HAMPTONS · LONG ISLAND
CHARDONNAY
1986 ESTATE RESERVE

This exquisite wine was estate grown, produced and bottled exclusively by The Bridgehampton Winery. Its elegant texture is the result of malolactic fermentation, which took place during the winter of 1986. Fermented and aged in two types of French oak—Nevers and Allier.

Alcohol 12.5% by vol. Contains sulfites.

THE BRIDGEHAMPTON WINERY, LONG ISLAND, NEW YORK 11932

to make fullbodied, buttery toasted wines, that develop with some bottle age. Alcohol levels tend to be higher in California than in Europe because all that extra sunshine produces sugar-rich grapes. Efforts are now being made to tone down the alcohol levels so that the wines are more elegant and subtle.

Sauvignon Blanc is often oak aged and sold as Fumé Blanc. Rhine Riesling, also called Johannisberg or White Riesling, is grown with some success. The wines tend to be heavier and fuller than their German counterparts, but there are some fine Late Harvest wines with honey and apricot flavours. Chenin Blanc and Gewürztraminer provide enjoyable drinking too.

New York State is the second wine producing state, with three main wine regions, the **Finger Lakes**, the **Hudson River Valley** and **Long Island**. The harsher climatic conditions of the Finger Lakes have meant that hardier vine varieties have been planted, as it was feared that *Vitis vinifera* would not survive the inclement winters. However, some tenacious growers succeed in producing Chardonnay and Riesling with some success.

Long Island has a milder maritime climate and although the industry is much newer than in the rest of the state – the first vineyards were planted in 1973 –Chardonnay and Merlot are beginning to make their mark.

The three states of **Oregon**, **Idaho** and **Washington** are collectively known as the Pacific Northwest. Oregon enjoys a cooler climate than California and may prove to be more successful for Pinot Noir and Riesling. Chardonnay and Cabernet Sauvignon grow there too, and the same system of AVAs and percentage regulations of grape varieties apply.

# SOUTH AMERICA

The wine production of South America is concentrated in Chile and Argentina. Some wine is also made in Brazil, Uruguay, and even Peru, but only for the home market. Argentina is the world's fifth largest wine producing country, but for political reasons her wines have lost the market share they enjoyed ten years ago, and are not generally available. However, this is our loss because wines made in Mendoza from Malbec and Cabernet show considerable potential. Thus it is in Chile that the interest in the South American wine industry is concentrated, a country of untapped potential about which we are certain to hear more.

The Andes dominate the geography and climate of Chile. They prevented the arrival of phylloxera so that the vines are ungrafted, while the melting

snows from the mountains provide essential water for irrigation. The valleys of the Aconcagua, Maipo, Cachapoal and Maule rivers, around Santiago are the main vineyard areas, with a climate tempered by the Pacific Ocean and the mountains.

White wines tend to be heavy and oxidized but, prompted by outside interest, are improving rapidly. Miguel Torres, the leading Spanish winemaker, is the prime mover in this trend towards cool fermentations to make fresh Rieslings, zingy Sauvignons and buttery Chardonnays. Others are following his example.

Red wines are more exciting, with Cabernet Sauvignon and Merlot blends undergoing some ageing in oak to produce serious wines. Chilean wine producers are still learning and some of the wine making is spoilt by an inability to combat the hot climate, but the potential is tremendous, with some rich fruity flavours of blackcurrants and cedarwood.

The most important criteria in choosing a Chilean wine are the producer's name and the grape variety. Sometimes a regional indication appears on the label, but many of the wineries are based near Santiago and may buy grapes from all over the country. Labels are in Spanish and popular terms, such as fino tinto, meaning fine red wine, and gran vino, have no legal basis and are merely indicative of the winemaker's conception of his wine.

### Chile

*An attractive colourful label of a Chilean scene, with the Andes that dominate the country's landscape.*

*Country of origin.*

*Name of winemaker given prominence. He established his reputation in Penedés, but is now making excellent wine in the southern hemisphere.*

MIGUEL TORRES
CHILE — M.R.

Santa Digna
Sauvignon Blanc

PRODUCED & BOTTLED BY VINICOLA MIGUEL TORRES LTDA
Panamericana Sur, km. 195 · CURICO · PRODUCT OF CHILE
Alc. by vol. 12·9%          Liquid content 750 c. c.

*Fantasy name for this white wine made from Sauvignon blanc*

*Self-explanatory information giving the name and address of the producer.*

*A wine company.*

# AUSTRALIA

$V$ines were brought to Australia by the first English settlers when they arrived at Botany Bay in 1788. Viticulture spread with the settlers through New South Wales, Victoria, South Australia, Western Australia and more recently to Tasmania. Until about twenty years ago the bulk of Australian wine production was concentrated on hefty fortified wines, port and sherry imitations. It is only since 1970 that there has been a definite shift towards lighter table wines. Australian wines have come into their own in the most exciting way.

Australian winemakers have a flexibility in their work which does not exist in Europe. They think nothing of buying grapes and trucking them in pressurized containers for a hundred miles or so from vineyard to winery. This means that the system of appellations is more or less anathema to Australians. What counts in the choice of an Australian wine is the name of the winery and the grape variety, or varietal, from which the wine is made.

Attempts to introduce an appellation system have so far been resisted, with two exceptions, **Mudgee** in the Upper Hunter and **Margaret River** in Western Australia. However, the appellation status is only an indication of provenance, that the wine in the bottle comes from grapes grown in that area, without any guarantee of quality. In fact, most Australian wine labels do give an area of origin which is generally a reliable guide. Often the label says the wine is estate grown and even gives a vineyard name. Part of the resistance to an appellation system arises because Australian winemakers are still finding out what grows well where and do not wish to impose restrictive regulations on a pioneering industry.

Australians have taken European grape varieties and adapted them to Australian conditions. Cabernet Sauvignon has been planted successfully, notably in Victoria's **Coonawarra**, to give rich, blackcurrant flavoured wines. Sometimes it is blended with Shiraz, the Syrah of the Rhône valley, or there is pure Shiraz, a warm spicy wine, which is at its best in the **Hunter Valley**. A grape variety on

*Taltarni*

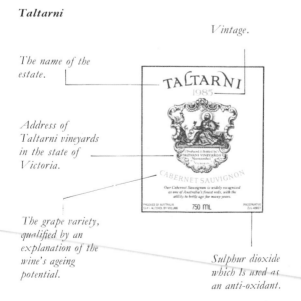

*Vintage.*

*The name of the estate.*

*Address of Taltarni vineyards in the state of Victoria.*

*The grape variety, qualified by an explanation of the wine's ageing potential.*

*Sulphur dioxide which is used as an anti-oxidant.*

## De Bortoli

The name of the producer.

The grape variety. De Bortoli have established a reputation for their Late Harvest Semillon. Late Harvest means that the grapes are left for longer on the vines so that they develop noble rot to make sweet wine.

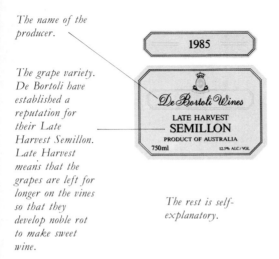

The rest is self-explanatory.

an Australian wine label means that the wine contains at least 80 per cent of that grape.

Most individual of the white varietals is Semillon, which comes into its own in the Hunter Valley, where it is usually matured in oak to give individual flavours with distinctive nutty overtones. Chardonnay is another popular varietal, with rich butter and pineapple flavours. Riesling is at its best in South Australia's **Barossa Valley**, brought here by German settlers in the 1840s and now grown successfully on cooler hill sites. Sometimes Riesling, and also Semillon, is Late Harvest and affected by *botrytis*, in which case the label says so.

A brief regional summary begins with the Hunter Valley in New South Wales. This is one of the hottest regions of Australia, where they make particularly successful Semillon, also known as Hunter Riesling. The Shiraz is good too. The nearby cooler Mudgee district is more important for Cabernet Sauvignons which are less successful in the Hunter Valley.

The most important vineyards of Victoria are in the northwest part of the state, where white grape varieties have been planted in high altitude vineyards with cool growing conditions. **Rutherglen, Corowa, Glenrowan, Milawa, Goulburn Valley, Yarra Valley, Geelong, Avoca** and **Great Western** are all names of areas that may feature on a label.

South Australia is best known for the Barossa Valley, which is the biggest wine area in the whole continent. Here Rhine Riesling is at its best. The nearby area of **Clare** produces similar juicy Rieslings. Coonawarra, to the south, is more important for red wines, while near Adelaide, **Southern Vales, Langhorne Creek** and **McLaren Vale** make good reds and whites.

The vineyards of Western Australia are nearly as old as those in the eastern part of the continent. The climate is extreme here, with hot and cool climate vineyards. Margaret River and **Mount Barker** are the two principal areas.

The trend in Australia is now very much towards the more elegant wines born of a cooler climate and, for this reason, viticulture has spread to temperate Tasmania. The wines are relatively unknown but promise well for the future.

Australian wines are amongst the most successful of the New World. The winemakers use modern technology, but the wines have a subtlety and nuance which are sometimes lacking in other New World wines.

Australian winemakers have a great love of back labels, which give the whole history of the wine, from the date of picking through every detail of the vinification process.

There are a few established outstanding wines such as Penfolds Grange Hermitage. Other names which have already established a reputation such as Rosemount, Brown Bros, Lindemans and Wynns are reliable and represent good value. Less well known names are definitely worth exploring.

# NEW ZEALAND

*T*he wines of New Zealand are amongst the most exciting new arrivals on our shelves. Everything has happened there within the last ten years. Talk to a New Zealand winemaker and he may tell you that he planted his Chardonnay as recently as 1982, or his Cabernet in 1984. Although wine has been made in New Zealand since the days of the early settlers, it is only in this decade that New Zealand wines have gained international recognition.

There are vineyards in both the North and South Islands. The first vines were planted at **Hawke's Bay** in North Island. It is now one of the largest wine areas together with **Gisborne** and **Auckland**,

and **Marlborough** and other nascent vineyards in South Island. These names may appear on a label, although as yet New Zealand has no precise system of appellations.

The great advantage in New Zealand is its cool climate, which gives lighter, more fragrant wines than some of the other New World countries. White wines are particularly successful. Most New Zealand wines are labelled by grape variety which implies a minimum of 75 per cent, or two grape varieties may feature, again provided they do not total less than 75 per cent. Sauvignon has a depth and subtlety of flavour which can compete with the Loire valley. Chardonnay is often matured in oak, with gentle, buttery overtones. Gewürztraminer is light and spicy, Riesling honeyed and Chenin Blanc fruity, while Müller Thurgau makes everyday quaffing wines. Red wines, too, are beginning to take on more stature, with some serious Cabernet Sauvignon, Merlot and Pinot Noir. The potential is fantastic.

### Montana

Name of the producer.

The vineyard area in New Zealand.

The grape variety.

Further descriptive information about the wine.

An address for Montana Wines and the name and address of their British importers.

# ENGLAND
# AND WALES

*E*nglish and Welsh wines deserve more attention than they are often given. Most people do not realize that vines have been grown in this country since Roman times, that viticulture flourished in the Middle Ages under the auspices of the monasteries. Over the last ten or fifteen years it has undergone something of a renaissance due to a renewed interest in English wine. However, the climate will always remain a serious obstacle to all but the most dedicated winemakers.

Vineyards are scattered over the south of England from East Anglia to Cornwall. The grape varieties are principally Germanic: Müller Thurgau, Huxelrebe, Reichensteiner, etc., and some hybrid varieties like Seyve Villard. A couple of producers persist with Pinot Noir, but with limited success. Most English wines follow the German taste, with light fragrant, slightly flowery flavours. They are usually light in alcohol, high in acidity, and, as in Germany, slightly sweet if sweet reserve is used.

In the eyes of the Common Market, English wine is no more than mere table wine, since grape varieties, not permitted in quality wines, are grown here. However, the English Vineyard Association has instituted its own system of awarding an annual quality seal, following tasting and analysis. The choice of an English wine is determined by the grape variety and the producer. The address of the winery on the label tells you which part of the country it comes from, although there are no significant regional differences.

A distinction must be made between English and British wine. English and Welsh wines are the products of grapes grown in those countries, unlike British wine which is manufactured from concentrated must imported from abroad, often from Cyprus or South Africa. There is no comparison between the two products.

### Pilton Manor

*A decorative label, playing upon the vineyard's historic origins.*

*The name of the vineyard.*

*The grape variety.*

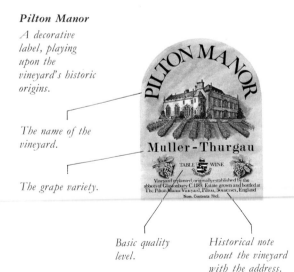

*Basic quality level.*

*Historical note about the vineyard with the address.*

# SOUTH AFRICA

$M$ost of the vineyards of South Africa centre upon Cape Town. They have been divided into seventeen official districts, entitled to the mention Wine of Origin, while some of the larger ones have in turn been subdivided into wards, the names of which also feature on a wine label.

The coastal region covering the land between the Atlantic Ocean and the Cape consists of the districts of **Constantia**, **Durbanville**, **Stellenbosch**, **Paarl**, **Tulbagh**, and **Swartland**. The region enjoys a relatively cool climate and produces some of the country's best table wines, especially Stellenbosch and Paarl. The warmer Breede River valley includes **Worcester**, **Robertson** and **Swellendam**, while the **Boberg** Region, which is synonymous with the districts of Paarl and Tulbagh, covers only fortified wine. In addition you may find **Overberg**, **Olifantsrivier**, **Piketberg**, **Klein-Karoo**, **Benede-Orange**, **Douglas** and **Andalusia**. Wines of Origin also bear a seal, with coloured bands on the capsule of the bottle. A blue band indicates that 100 per cent of the wine comes from the indicated region; a red band that 75 per cent of the wine comes from the vintage on the label, and a green band that the wine contains the legal minimum of the particular grape variety—usually 75 per cent. The words 'estate wine' on a label certifies that the wine was produced from grapes grown on that estate. An additional qualification of 'superior' is given to wines of exceptional quality, equating them to a premier cru in the French appellation system.

The percentages allow for a certain flexibility in blending and in fact many of the popular South African wines, such as the KWV's Roodeberg, are

### Stellenbosch

*Wine labels in South Africa are bilingual, in Afrikaans as well as English.*

*Brand name occasionally used by Stellenbosch Farmers. Also the name of the farm of one of South Africa's early winemakers, where the Stellenbosch Farmers now have their headquarters.*

*Origin Stellenbosch.*

*South African term for the Riesling of Germany.*

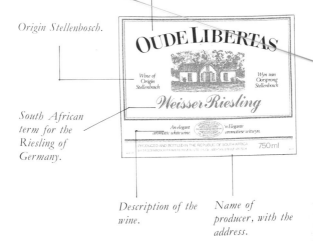

*Description of the wine.*

*Name of producer, with the address.*

blends which do not conform to the system.

The choice of grape variety, or cultivar, is the prime factor in selecting a South African wine. European varieties such as Cabernet Sauvignon, ...t, Sauvignon Blanc and Chenin Blanc, which ...mes called Steen, have all been planted in ...h some success. A popular cultivar i ...d of Pinot Noir and Cinsaut. Rhi... ...Weisser Riesling and may ...t if the grapes are picked ...cted by noble rot. Speci... ...est is also permitted.

# SPARKLING WINES

*T*he bubbles of carbon dioxide in a bottle of sparkling wine are the result of a second fermentation, which may take place in the bottle or the vat. The one exception to this is carbonated wine, which is injected with carbon dioxide.

No one disputes that **champagne** is the greatest of all sparkling wines, a unique combination of grape varieties and soil which produces wines with a delicate individual flavour. The grape varieties in question are Pinot Noir, Pinot Meunier and Chardonnay. The champagne method has evolved out of the need to remove the sediment resulting from the second fermentation in the bottle.

The base wine is made in the normal way and when it is bottled, yeast and sugar are added to induce the second fermentation. When this is complete the wine must spend a minimum of twelve months on the lees of the fermentation in order to take on an extra dimension of flavour. The bottles are then put horizontally into wooden racks, or *pupitres*, and the process of remuage carried out, in which the bottles are gently twisted each day to encourage the offending sediment to settle on the capsule. When the process is complete the bottles are vertical, but upside down. To disgorge them, their necks are frozen, so that a pellet of ice containing the sediment can be removed easily. The bottles are then topped up with wine and a dosage of sugar, which determines the degree of sweetness in the champagne. The terms are, in ascending order of sweetness, extra brut, with no dosage; brut, which is most common; extra sec; semi sec and doux. Most champagne is non-vintage, a blend of several years. In theory a vintage champagne wine of one year alone, is only made in the best years. In practice these occur with increasing frequency, so that someone makes a vintage wine in most years. Whereas for non-vintage champagne, the wine must spend a minimum of twelve months on the lees of the second fermentation from the January after the harvest, this period is increased to three years for a vintage wine. Another style of champagne is crémant, which sparkles less briskly than normal champagne. (Crémant in other appellations is a straightforward sparkler.) Vineyards are classified grand or premier cru which is sometimes mentioned on the label.

Saumur in the Loire valley is the other important source of French sparkling wine. The champagne method was introduced to the region in the early 19th century by Jean Ackerman. The chalk hills

## Champagne

*The name of the producer, in Reims, France, displayed prominently as this is the most significant factor in choosing a bottle of champagne. They supply the Queen, hence the royal warrant.*

*A pink champagne.*

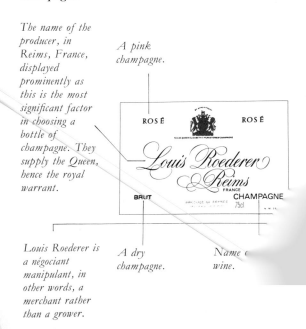

*Louis Roederer is a négociant manipulant, in other words, a merchant rather than a grower.*

*A dry champagne.*

*Name of wine.*

around Saumur provide excellent cellars and the Chenin Blanc, with its firm point of acidity, adapts readily to the champagne technique. Sparkling Saumur is labelled as Saumur Mousseux and may be qualified as sec, demi-sec or doux. A pink version is also made. The same goes for sparkling Anjou and both may be pétillant, or less sparkling. There is also a sparkling version of Vouvray and Montlouis.

A champagne label simply says champagne. That is enough. You know immediately the provenance of the wine and the method of production. But sparkling wines produced in this way in other areas are, for the present, allowed to tell you that they use the methode champenoise. However, from September 1994 this will no longer be permitted on a label and the wording is gradually being changed. Traditional method is deemed an acceptable alternative, as is classical method, which is the same as the Italian metodo classico. **Crémant d'Alsace**, **Crémant de Bourgogne**, **Crémant de la Loire** and **Blanquette de Limoux** automatically mean the champagne method, as imperative to the appellation. Other French sparkling wines have to state their method of production.

The Spanish sparkling wine **Cava** also implies a champagne method wine, as an essential part of the DO. Most Cava comes from Penedés in northern Spain. Usually it is dry, but like champagne has a range of flavours which are indicated on the label as follows: extra brut; brut; extra seco, which is off-dry rather than very dry; semi seco, more semi-sweet than semi-dry; and dulce which is very sweet. Extra brut and brut are the most common.

Germany plain **Sekt** or **Schaumwein** means the grapes have come from outside Germany. This kind of wine used to be called **Deutscher Sekt** even if made in Germany, but happily, since 1986, German Sekt must derive only from German grapes, with a minimum age of ten months. However, the better German sparkling wines are qualified by an area of production, meaning that a minimum of 85 per cent of the grapes come from the region given on the label. Much German Sekt is made by the cuve close or charmat method of production, whereby the second fermentation takes place in a tank so that the resulting sediment is filtered away under pressure, removing the need for the expensive processes of remuage and dégorgement. An intermediary way, also used in Germany, is the transfer method where the second fermentation takes place in the bottle, the wine subsequently being decanted into a vat for filtration. The words Flaschengärung, or bottle fermented, indicate this, while the German term for the champagne method is 'Flaschengärung nach dem traditionellen Verfahren'. The best German sparkling wines are based on the Riesling grape.

The most famous sparkling wine of Italy is **Asti Spumante**, a deliciously grapey, sweet bubbly wine made from the Muscat grape. It goes better with wedding cake than many a dry champagne. For the best Asti the method of production is neither that of champagne nor of charmat. The first fermentation is stopped by chilling the juice to retain some of the natural sweetness of the grapes, which is then allowed to re-ferment after bottling.

There is also an increasing volume of good dry sparkling wine from Italy, particularly from the north, made by the champagne method and labelled either metodo champenoise, until 1994, or metodo classico. Various DOCs include a spumante or slightly less bubbly, frizzante version. The popular Lambrusco is lightly sparkling and labelled frizzante. The method is charmat.

The words spumante in Italy, mousseux in France and espumoso in Spain will be qualified accordingly if the wine is made by the champagne method. Simple vin mousseux without any indication of method, automatically implies the cuve close method.

The New World has a cavalier attitude towards the use of the word champagne. Both Australia and California are important producers of sparkling wine, partly motivated by interest and investment from champagne producers such as Domaine Chandon in the Napa Valley, to cite but one. In America and Australia any sparkling wine may be called champagne, irrespective of the method of production. However, if these are to be imported into the Common Market, they must be content with being called sparkling wine. Bottle fermented implies the transfer method of production, while 'fermentation in this bottle' is the clue to the champagne method.

The moral is to read the small print carefully. Cheap sparkling wine will often try to look like champagne but, if there is no mention of the word champagne on the label, it is not champagne.

### Champagne method

There is no area of origin, other than produce of Italy, and therefore no Denominazione. In buying this wine, you are placing your confidence in Antinori's expertise as a producer.

Very dry.

Name of producer, prominently displayed as for a champagne label.

Meaning traditional champagne method and amplified with the explanation that it is a quality sparkling wine, fermented in this bottle and disgorged in the autumn of 1987.

Produced and bottled in San Casciano Val di Pesa, where Antinori have their production plant.

# FORTIFIED WINES

*F*ortified wine is the general term for a wine that requires the addition of brandy at some stage during its production process. Port and sherry are the most common fortified wines and, as they have been imitated outside Spain and Portugal, it is more logical to compare and contrast their labels and tastes, irrespective of country of origin.

True sherry comes from Spain, but you can find imitations in South Africa and Cyprus, as well as Australia, not to mention a concocted product called British sherry, about which the less said the better. Sherry from Spain says simply sherry on the label. Cyprus and Britain are still allowed to call their wine sherry, but qualified by its origin, for example, Cyprus Sherry. On the other hand, Australia has never used the term sherry, and since the entry of Spain into the Common Market, South Africa has been forbidden to use it too.

Authentic sherry covers an exciting range of flavours from the austerely dry to the lusciously sweet. The driest, **Fino** sherry, results from a curious *flor*, or layer of yeast which develops in the cask during the period of maturation, giving it a distinctive dry tang. **Manzanilla** is similarly dry, but only comes from wine aged in the town of Sanlúcar de Barrameda.

Next in the scale of sweetness comes **Amontillado**, which loosely refers to a medium-dry sherry, whereas true Amontillado is an aged Fino. **Oloroso**, meaning fragrant, can be either sweet or dry, but is always darker and richer than other sherries. Oloroso is also sweetened to make Cream Sherry or left as a mature dry wine of deep colour and intense flavour. **Pale Cream** sherry, as its name implies, is a

## Sherry

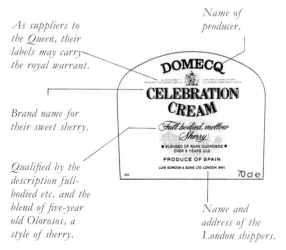

*Name of producer.*

*As suppliers to the Queen, their labels may carry the royal warrant.*

*Brand name for their sweet sherry.*

*Qualified by the description full-bodied etc. and the blend of five-year old Olorosos, a style of sherry.*

DOMECQ

**CELEBRATION CREAM**

*Full bodied, mellow Sherry*

★ BLENDED OF RARE OLOROSOS ★ OVER 5 YEARS OLD

**PRODUCE OF SPAIN**

LUIS GORDON & SONS LTD. LONDON SW1.

202                    70 cl e

*Name and address of the London shippers.*

colourless sweet sherry, with an appearance remarkably like Fino, so check the label. **Palo Cortado** is an unusual cross between Amontillado and Oloroso.

Occasionally the term almacenista is seen on a sherry label. It describes somebody who matures wine on a small scale, but does not actually make it. The company Emilio Lustau has made a feature of selling such wines, calling them almacenista.

The other important aspect of sherry production is the solera system. This is a method of maturing wine, which depends upon the fact that a young wine, when blended with a larger quantity of old wine, immediately takes on the characteristics of the older wine. Sherry is never a vintage wine and any date on the label will refer to the commencement of a solera.

The solera system features in two other Spanish wines, **Montilla** and **Málaga**. Montilla is lighter with less bite, as it is often unfortified. Málaga, made from the Moscatel grape, is usually sweet and rich. It is labelled according to its sweetness, from seco to dulce, and its colour, with blanco, dorado, rojo—

dorado, oscuro and negro, meaning respectively, white, golden, tawny, dark and black.

Portugal has given the world three fortified wines, madeira, port and **Moscatel de Setúbal**, of which port is easily the most popular. The name port is more rigorously protected than that of sherry, so while there are port-style wines in the New World, notably Australia, California and South Africa, they have never been labelled as such, but merely as tawny or ruby, or some such name to imply a similarity to their Portuguese counterpart.

The Douro valley is the home of port. Here sturdy vines grow on wild rugged hillsides and produce wines which require extensive bottle age. The best port of all is **vintage port**, made only in exceptional years, when the wine requires several years maturation in bottle before it is palatable. Vintage port is not the same as **Late-Bottled Vintage** (LBV). Read the label carefully to avoid confusion. An LBV is a means of producing a less expensive wine of vintage character, with the cachet of a date, which is not a declared vintage year. It comes from a wine bottled between four and a half and six years after the harvest, so it has matured in wood, whereas true vintage port is bottled after its second winter. The other occasion when a port bottle carries a date is when the wine is from a single estate or *quinta*, such as Quinta da Vargellas. The name of the *quinta* is always on the label. Again, such a wine is not made in a declared vintage year.

Port necessitates ageing in wood. Cheap **ruby** spends three or four years in barrel, as does cheap **tawny**, which may well be a blend of red and white port. However, the best tawny ports may spend as long as thirty or forty years in wood, so that the red colour of the young wine fades to a brick tawny colour. If the label states twenty year old tawny, it is a blend of wines with an average age of twenty, a deliciously nutty drink, redolent of liquid walnuts. Young white port makes an original aperitif.

## Port

*A sober label, befitting to vintage port.*

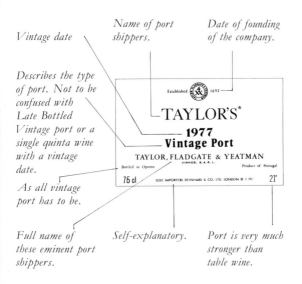

Name of port shippers.

Date of founding of the company.

Vintage date

Describes the type of port. Not to be confused with Late Bottled Vintage port or a single quinta wine with a vintage date.

As all vintage port has to be.

Full name of these eminent port shippers.

Self-explanatory.

Port is very much stronger than table wine.

Established 1692

**TAYLOR'S**®
**1977**
**Vintage Port**
TAYLOR, FLADGATE & YEATMAN
VINHOS, S.A.R.L.

Bottled in Oporto

Product of Portugal

76 cl

SOLE IMPORTERS DEINHARD & CO. LTD. LONDON SE 1 7XT

21°

Madeira, from the volcanic island in the Atlantic Ocean, requires a particular production process, whereby the wine is cooked in a sealed oven or *estufa*, to give it a distinctive taste. This unique method of vinification was developed when it was realized that wine used as ballast on the long voyage to India was greatly improved after crossing the Equator. Thus the modern *estufa* system imitates the cooking process which took place in the ship's hold. Four basic styles of madeira are made, from dry to sweet, **Sercial**, **Verdelho**, **Bual** and **Malmsey**, all based on grape varieties of the same name. The first two are best as an aperitif, the last two ideal after dinner drinks, instead of port.

Madeira is a blended wine. It must have a minimum age of three years, while a reserve wine is matured for five years and a special reserve for ten

## Madeira

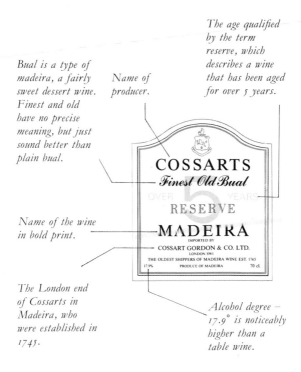

*The age qualified by the term reserve, which describes a wine that has been aged for over 5 years.*

*Bual is a type of madeira, a fairly sweet dessert wine. Finest and old have no precise meaning, but just sound better than plain bual.*

*Name of producer.*

**COSSARTS**
*Finest Old Bual*

RESERVE

**MADEIRA**
IMPORTED BY
COSSART GORDON & CO. LTD.
LONDON SW1
THE OLDEST SHIPPERS OF MADEIRA WINE EST. 1745
17.9%          PRODUCE OF MADEIRA          70 cl.

*Name of the wine in bold print.*

*The London end of Cossarts in Madeira, who were established in 1745.*

*Alcohol degree – 17.9° is noticeably higher than a table wine.*

years. A vintage wine, which is quite rare, must be aged for a minimum of twenty years in wood. A solera system is sometimes used, but this is rarer than for sherry. However, there is no doubt that madeira is the most long-lived of all wines.

Moscatel de Setúbal, as the name implies, is a fortified wine made principally from the Moscatel grape, grown on the Setúbal peninsular near Lisbon.

Marsala is the characteristic Italian fortified wine produced in Sicily. Cheap marsala, is used for making zabaglione, but regulations have now been tightened and there are several permitted categories: fine, superiore, riserva, vergine and stravecchia. The colour can be oro, ambra or rubino–in other words golden, amber or ruby, and the flavour may be secco, semi secco or dolce.

France is the land of vin doux naturel, or naturally sweet wines, which are fortified to retain their natural sugar from the grape. Most popular is Muscat de Beaumes-de-Venise. There are other wines made from Muscat in the south of France, such as **Muscat de Frontignan**, **Lunel** and **Rivesaltes**. At their best they are deliciously fresh and grapey. **Rivesaltes**, **Banyuls**, **Maury** and **Rasteau** are based on the black Grenache grape and may be France's answer to port, as rich raisiny dessert wines.

California has the occasional fortified dessert wine, made from Muscat, as well as some port imitations. But it is Australia which makes the best fortified wine outside Europe, with her delicious **Liqueur Muscat** made from overripe grapes in Rutherglen in Victoria.

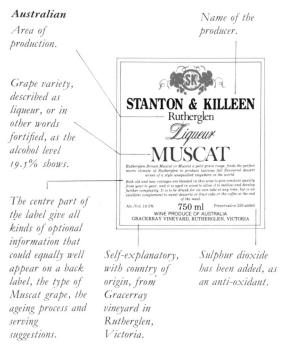

*Australian*

*Area of production.*

*Name of the producer.*

*Grape variety, described as liqueur, or in other words fortified, as the alcohol level 19.5% shows.*

*The centre part of the label give all kinds of optional information that could equally well appear on a back label, the type of Muscat grape, the ageing process and serving suggestions.*

*Self-explanatory, with country of origin, from Gracerray vineyard in Rutherglen, Victoria.*

*Sulphur dioxide has been added, as an anti-oxidant.*

# VINTAGES

**1988** It may have been a wet summer in Britain, but in France and Germany the sun shone. Outstanding wines were made in Germany, Alsace, Bordeaux, Burgundy, Piedmont and Tuscany. The weather obliged in Sauternes, too. Australia was unlucky.

**1987** A mixed year, needing a careful choice of wine in most areas. Beaujolais is one of the most successful French appellations; Chablis is sound; bordeaux and burgundy will be short-lived. A few good German QmPs, and from Spain Penedés is excellent.

**1986** Some excellent claret and good Sauternes. White burgundies are better than red, with good Chablis. Germany was average, Italy likewise.

**1985** Some excellent claret, making for long-lived wines. Red burgundies will be great, and whites very fine. Beaujolais too, is good. A champagne vintage for most houses, and a vintage for some port shippers. Good Rhône wines; excellent Alsace and some great Chianti riservas and Barolo.

**1984** Rather a dull year, with only average quality bordeaux and burgundy, without any staying power. The same goes for the Rhône and Germany. Tuscany was a washout.

**1983** Some great claret and Sauternes. Excellent red burgundies, and Beaujolais; rich whites, including Chablis. Some outstanding Alsace and German wines. Fruity Chianti. Good Rhône and sweet Loire wines. A champagne vintage, and a port vintage for some shippers.

**1982** Rich powerful claret; less successful Sauternes. Difficult for red burgundy; whites are better. Some good Rhônes. A champagne and a port vintage. Good Chianti and Barolo. Average Germans.

**1981** Light but good claret. White Burgundy better than red, with excellent Chablis. Some good Alsace. Rhônes need careful selection. A few good Germans.

**1980** A dull year, apart from a port vintage. Wines without staying power in Bordeaux and Burgundy, requiring careful selection. Better than average Rhônes.

---

Vintages to look out for from the 70s and earlier:

Claret – 1978 – 1970 – 1966 – 1962 and 1961

Red burgundy – 1978 – 1971 – 1969 – 1966

White burgundy and Chablis – 1978 – 1975 – 1971

Sauternes – 1978 – 1976 – 1975 – 1971 – 1967

Germany – 1976 – 1975 – 1971

Alsace – 1976

Rhône – 1978

Sweet Loire – 1976 – 1975 – 1971 – 1964

Vintage port – 1977 still too young to drink, 1975 – 1970, 1967, 1966, 1963, 1960

Champagne – 1979 – 1976 – 1975 – 1971

Piedmont – 1978 – 1974 – 1971

Tuscany – 1979 – 1977 – 1975 – 1971

# GLOSSARY

**Abboccato** Italian for medium dry.

**Abfüllung** German for bottling.

**Abocado** Spanish for medium sweet.

**Abymes** white wine of Savoie.

**Acidity** an essential component of all wine, present in different forms, mainly tartaric, citric, lactic and malic. Without acidity a wine would be flat and flabby; with too much it would taste green and sharp. Volatile acidity, of which acetic acid, as in vinegar, is the most important, should be kept to a minimum.

**Adamado** Portuguese for sweet.

**Adega** Portuguese for cellar or producer.

**Ahr** German QbA area.

**Ajaccio** AC of Corsica.

**Alentejo** wine region of Portugal.

**Alexander Valley** Californian AVA.

**Aligoté** white grape variety grown principally in Burgundy for the appellation Bourgogne Aligoté. Makes crisp dry wine for early drinking.

**Almacenista** see sherry.

**Alto Adige** wine region of northern Italy.

**Amabile** Italian for medium sweet.

**Amaro** Italian for bitter.

**Amarone** a type of Valpolicella made from dried grapes fermented until no sugar remains. A rich fullbodied wine.

**Amontillado** a medium sweet sherry.

**Amoroso** sweet oloroso sherry, now rarely seen.

**Anejado por** Spanish for aged by.

**Anjou** AC of the Loire valley.

**Annata** Italian for vintage.

**Appellation Contrôlée** see France.

**Apremont** white wine of Savoie.

**Arbois** AC of the Jura.

**Asciutto** Italian for dry.

**Assemblage** French term for blending. In Bordeaux it refers to the blending of different grape varieties. In Champagne the wine is made from an assemblage of vineyards and years, as well as grape varieties. The sum of the component parts is better than any single part.

**Asti Spumante** sweet Italian sparkling wine.

**Ausbruch** Austrian term indicating a level of sweetness between Beerenauslese and Trockenbeerenauslese, in other words very sweet.

**Auslese** the third category of German Prädikat wines, meaning literally 'selected harvest'. The winemaker chooses bunches of grapes which are especially ripe or affected with noble rot, so that the resulting wine will be sweet and honeyed. Also used in Austria and Italy's Alto Adige.

**Authorized Viticultural Area (AVA)** *see* North America.

**Azienda** Italian for farm. Often seen on labels as Azienda Agricola, meaning 'company owning vineyards', or Azienda Vinicola meaning 'estate winery'.

**Baden** QbA of southern Germany.

**Bairrada** up and coming Portuguese wine.

**Bandol** best red wine of Provence.

**Banyuls** VDN from southern France.

**Barbaresco** fine northern Italian red DOCG.

**Barbera** a red grape variety planted mainly in northwest Italy, making wines with fresh acidity for early drinking.

**Bardolino** red wine of northern Italy.

**Barolo** great northern Italian red DOCG.

**Barossa Valley** Australian wine region.

**Barsac** Bordeaux AC for sweet white wine.

**Beaujolais** easiest-to-drink burgundy from Gamay grape.

**Beerenauslese** fourth category of German Prädikat wine, meaning 'a selection of berries' which have been affected by noble rot. It is only made in the very best years, such as 1988, and will develop with bottle age.

**Bellet** small AC of Provence.

**Bereich** a subregion of German vineyards, grouping vineyards of similar character and taking its name from the most important village in the area, eg, Bereich Bernkastel which covers the Middle Mosel.

**Bergerac** AC of southwest France.

**Bergwein** term used in Austria to describe wine produced from steep hillsides.

**Bernkastel** wine town on the Mosel.

**Beyaz** Turkish for white.

**Bianco** Italian for white.

**Bijelo** Yugoslav for white.

# GLOSSARY

**Blanc** French for white.

**Blanc de Blancs** white wine made from white grapes, which nearly all white wine is, champagne being a notable exception. The term is often used for French table wine to make it sound better than it is. Champagne made only from Chardonnay may also be labelled Blanc de Blancs.

**Blanc de Noirs** white wine made from red grapes, such as a champagne made only from Pinot Noir.

**Blanco** Spanish for white.

**Blanquette de Limoux** sparkling wine from the Midi.

**Blush wine** a fashionable term for a pink wine.

**Bodega** Spanish for a wine cellar and a company making wine.

**Bonnezeaux** sweet white Loire AC.

**Bourgueil** red Loire AC.

**Bourgogne** *see* Burgundy.

**Branco** Portuguese for white.

**British wine** a wine produced in Britain from reconstituted concentrated grape must. Not to be confused with English wine.

**Brunello di Montalcino** fine Tuscan red DOGC.

**Brut** very dry, with the lowest dosage, in Champagne; also used in Italy and Spain to describe a dry sparkling wine.

**Bruto** Portuguese equivalent of brut.

**Bual** one of the four styles of madeira, not as sweet as Malmsey, but usually rich enough to be drunk as a dessert wine.

**Bull's Blood** Hungarian red wine.

**Burgenland** wine region of Austria.

**Buzet** mainly red AC of southwest France.

**CM** on a champagne label, means the wine has been made by a cooperative.

**Cabernet Franc** a red grape variety at its most characteristic in the Loire valley, making wines such as Chinon and Bourgueil. It is also important in Bordeaux, especially in St-Emilion. Also grown in north Italy where Cabernet may mean a blend of Franc and Sauvignon.

**Cabernet Sauvignon** the world's greatest red grape variety, responsible for a significant part of the blend of the Médoc and the Graves, which has successfully adapted to the New World, notably California and Australia. Benefits from ageing in wood and can achieve wines of considerable longevity.

**Cahors** good red AC from southwest France.

**Cantina** Italian for cellar.

**Cantina Sociale** a wine cooperative in Italy.

**Carbonated wine** wine into which carbon dioxide has been injected to give it a sparkle. The bubbles are short-lived once the bottle has been opened.

**Carignan** a red grape variety grown extensively in the Midi, gradually being replaced by better grape varieties.

**Carmignano** Tuscan red DOC.

**Carneros Creek** Californian AVA.

**Casa Vinicola** Italian wine producer who purchases grapes.

**Cascina** Italian for farm, sometimes appears on a label.

**Cassis** white Provence AC.

**Casta** Portuguese for grape variety.

**Castello** Italian for castle—often part of the estate name on a label.

**Cava** Spanish for sparkling wine made by the champagne method. A DO in its own right. The best come from Penedés.

**Cave** French for cellar.

**Cave Coopérative** cooperative cellar in France.

**Cepa** Spanish for grape variety, occasionally used in the same way as cépage in France.

**Cépage** French for grape variety, may appear on the label to qualify a single grape variety.

**Cerasuolo** Italian term to describe a light red or dark pink wine, as in Cerasuolo di Vittorio.

**Chablis** white wine of northern Burgundy.

**Champagne Method** the method of making sparkling wine developed in the Champagne region of France, imitated all over the world. The second fermentation must take place in the bottle in which the wine is sold, entailing the processes of remuage and dégorgement to remove the sediment, and including a period of maturation on the second fermentation's lees. The addition of some sugar, the dosage, at the moment of dégorgement determines the level of the wine's sweetness.

**Chaptalization** a means of increasing the alcohol level in wine by adding sugar to the fermenting must in order that the yeast has more sugar to convert into alcohol. The process is strictly controlled and forbidden altogether in the warmer parts of France. However, in cooler areas it can make for a better balanced wine.

**Chardonnay** grape variety used for making most white burgundy. It has adapted well in other parts of Europe and the New World, notably in Australia and California. It benefits from vinification in oak and some bottle age. It is an important part of a champagne blend.

**Charmat** another name for the cuve close method of producing sparkling wine.

**Château** literally means 'castle' in French, but is used, especially in Bordeaux, to describe a wine estate. The château may be a large mansion or a small farmhouse. Vins de pays may not use the term, even if there is a château on the property.

**Château-bottled** the wine is bottled at the château, not by a merchant.

**Château-Chalon** Jura AC for Vin Jaune.

**Château Grillet** tiny white AC of northern Rhône.

**Château Musar** principal estate of the Lebanon.

**Châteauneuf-du-Pape** AC of southern Rhône.

**Chenin Blanc** a white grape at its best in the Loire valley where it shows great versatility, producing not only still and sparkling wines but also the whole range of tastes from very dry to very sweet, always with a firm backbone of acidity. Found also in the New World, notably New Zealand and South Africa.

**Chianti** the principal red wine of Tuscany.

**Chiaretto** Italian for a pale red wine notably in Bardolino.

**Chinon** red AC of the Loire valley.

**Cinsaut** a red grape variety grown extensively in the Midi, usually blended with Grenache and Carignan.

**Clairette de Die** sparkling wine of the Rhône valley.

**Claret** traditional English term for red bordeaux.

**Clarete** Spanish and Portuguese for light red wine; opposite to tinto.

**Classical Method** new term to describe the champagne method.

**Classico** Italian term for vineyards at the heart of a region; considered to produce the best wine, eg. Chianti Classico.

**Clos** literally means a 'walled vineyard' in French, often part of a Burgundian vineyard name, even after the walls have disappeared, eg. Clos de Vougeot.

**Cold Fermentation** fermentation conducted at a lower than usual temperature, at about 17–18°C, especially for white wine. As wine cellars are modernized this is becoming increasingly common in hotter climates such as the Midi.

**Cold Stabilization Treatment** a method of removing tartrate crystals from wine. Wine is chilled to minus 5°C for about a week, which causes the tartaric acid in it to precipitate so that the tartrate crystals may be filtered out of the wine before bottling.

**Colheita** Portuguese for vintage.

**Collio** DOC of northeast Italy.

**Collioure** fullbodied red AC of the Midi.

**Commandaria** traditional dessert wine of Cyprus.

**Condrieu** distinctive white AC of northern Rhône.

**Consorzio** a voluntary growers' association in Italy.

**Constantia** South African wine region.

**Coonawarra** important Australian wine region.

**Corbières** mainly red AC of the Midi.

**Cornas** red AC of northern Rhône.

**Corton** fine red burgundy.

**Corvo** Sicilian table wine.

**Cosecha** Spanish for vintage.

**Costières du Gard** AC of the Midi.

**Côte** French for hill or slope. Most of the better French vineyards are on slopes; a word often incorporated into French wine names, eg. Côte de Beaune.

**Côte Chalonnaise** *see* Burgundy.

**Côte de Beaune** part of the Côte d'Or.

**Côte de Nuit** part of the Côte d'Or.

**Côte d'Or** *see* Burgundy.

**Côte Roannaise** red VDQS of the Loire.

**Côte Rôtie** fine red AC of northern Rhône.

**Coteau** French for hillside. A word often incorporated into French wine names.

**Coteaux d'Aix-en-Provence** AC of Provence.

**Coteaux de Mascara** Algerian AC.

**Coteaux de Tricastin** AC of central Rhône.

**Coteaux du Languedoc** large AC of the Midi.

**Coteaux du Layon** sweet AC of Loire.

**Coteaux Varois** VDQS of Provence.

**Côtes de Duras** AC of southwest France

**Côtes de Provence** large AC of Provence

**Côtes du Forez** red VDQS of the Loire.

**Côtes du Frontonnais** red AC of southwest France

**Côtes du Jura** principal AC of the Jura.

**Côtes du Lubéron** AC of Provence.

**Côtes du Marmandais** VDQS of southwest France.

**Côtes du Rhône** large AC of the Rhône valley, mainly from the south.

**Côtes du Roussillon** AC of Midi.

**Côtes du Ventoux** AC of southern Rhône.

**Coulure** a disorder of the vine, adversely affecting its yield if the flowering takes place in unsatisfactory weather conditions. As a result the berries fail to develop. Grenache is particularly susceptible.

**Cream Sherry** the sweetest style of sherry.

**Crémant** in Champagne crémant has a slightly lower pressure than fully sparkling champagne, while in Alsace, Burgundy and the Loire it is fully sparkling like champagne.

**Crépy** white AC of Savoie.

**Criado por** on a Spanish label means matured and, possibly, blended for.

**Crianza** describes the ageing of a Rioja, con crianza means it has been matured for a minimum of twelve months in cask, and some months, usually six, in bottle and must not be sold before the third year after the vintage.

**Sin crianza** describes a young wine bottled during the year after the vintage.

**Crozes-Hermitage** mainly red AC of northern Rhône.

**Crno** Yugoslav for red.

**Cru** translates literally as 'growth', describing a vineyard of particular quality and status, often qualified by grand or premier.

**Cru Bourgeois** category below classed growth in the Médoc.

**Cru Classé** describes the châteaux of the Médoc which were classified in 1855.

**Cru Grand Bourgeois Exceptionnel** a superior cru bourgeois, which is always aged in wood and château bottled.

**Crusted port** a term no longer recognized in Portugal, but similar to vintage character port, a blend of different vineyards and years.

**Cuve close** method of producing sparkling wine whereby the second fermentation takes place in a vat so that the resulting sediment can be filtered out of the wine under pressure before bottling. It is much cheaper than the champagne method.

**Cuvée** in French the contents of a vat of wine. A word often qualified by spéciale or réserve to mean a special selection of wine.

Cuvée du patron often refers to a restaurant house wine.

**Dão** important Portuguese wine region.

**Dealcoholized wine** a wine which has had its natural alcohol removed to make it acceptable to those wishing to reduce their alcohol consumption. It may not always be so acceptable to their taste buds!

**Dégorgement** part of the champagne method, which entails the removal of the sediment from the second fermentation. Usually this is done by freezing the neck of the bottle, to remove an ice pellet of wine which contains the offending sediment.

**Demi-sec** French for medium dry.

**Denominazione di Origine Controlata** *see* Italy.

**Denominación de Origen** *see* Spain.

**Doce** Portuguese for sweet.

**Dolce** Italian for sweet.

**Dolcetto** Piedmontese grape variety making red wines for early drinking.

**Dôle** Swiss red wine.

**Domaine** French for wine estate.

**Dosage** the sugar added to a sparkling wine after dégorgement to determine the degree of sweetness, from Brut, Extra Sec, Sec, Demi Sec and Doux.

**Douro** Portuguese wine, region noted for port and table wine.

**Dry Creek** Californian AVA.

**Dulce** Spanish for sweet.

**Edelfäule** German for noble rot.

**Edelkeur** South African sweet wine, made from nobly rotten grapes.

**Edelzwicker** wine from a blend of grape varieties made in Alsace.

**Egrappage** French term for destalking grapes, a process which is increasingly common in red wine making as it reduces the tannin level making the wine ready for drinking earlier. However, the increasing use of mechanical harvesters has reduced the need for égrappage.

**Eiswein** Ice wine; a wine made in Germany from frozen grapes left on the vines until December or January. A curiosity.

**Elaborado por** Spanish for matured and/or blended for.

**Elevé en Fûts de Chêne** aged in oak barrels, mentioned on the label to add extra prestige to the wine, especially if they are *fûts neufs*, new barrels.

**Eltville** important wine village in the Rheingau.

**Embotellado por** Spanish for bottled for.

**Engarrafado na Origem**
Portuguese for estate
bottled.

**English Vineyards
Association** represents the
wine growers of the United
Kingdom and awards an
EVA seal, for display on the
bottle, to wines of the
required quality.

**Entre-Deux-Mers** Bordeaux
AC for dry white wine.

**Envasado en Origen** South
American for estate bottled.

**Erbach** wine village in the
Rheingau.

**Erzeugabfüllung** German
for estate bottled.

**Espumoso** Spanish for
sparkling wine.

**Estate Bottled** wine bottled
on the property where the
grapes were grown and the
wine vinified.

**Estate Wine** South African
term to indicate the wine
comes from grapes grown
and vinified on the estate.

**Estufa** the estufa system is
an essential part of the
production of madeira. In
the 16th century madeira was
used as ballast by ships
travelling to India, which
entailed crossings of the
Equator. The resulting heat
treatment benefited the wine
so much that it has been
imitated for all qualities of
madeira by the use of an
*estufa*, a special heated tank.
The process is carefully
controlled at a temperature
of 45°C, with 5° tolerance

each way. Three months is
the minimum period. Often
producers prefer a lower
temperature for as long as
six months. This cooking
process is responsible for the
unique flavours of madeira.

**Etoile** Jura AC for white
wine.

**Fattoria** Italian for an estate
or farm.

**Faugères** part of Coteaux du
Languedoc.

**Fehér** Hungarian for white.

**Fermentation** the
conversion of grape juice
into wine. Yeast feeds off
the sugar in the grapes,
transforming it into alcohol
and carbon dioxide.

**Fermentazione Naturale**
Italian for natural
fermentation, describing a
sparkling wine – made by a
natural refermentation in the
bottle.

**Filtration** the process of
clarification, usually just
before bottling, to remove
any suspended particles in
the wine, including yeast and
bacteria which may be
invisible to the naked eye.

**Finger Lakes** wine area of
New York State.

**Fining** the clarification of
wine, usually after the
fermentation has finished. A
substance is added which
attracts the tiny particles
suspended in the wine,
causing them to coagulate
and drop to the bottom of
the vat.

**Fino** the driest and most delicate of sherries, dependent on the development of *flor* for its characteristic taste. See *flor*.

**Fiore** the first pressing of juice, translating literally as 'flower' in Italian. An indication of quality.

**Fitou** red AC of the Midi.

**Flaschengärung** bottle fermentation, for a sparkling wine in Germany.

**Fleurie** Beaujolais cru.

**Flor** the film of saccharamyces yeast which develops on the surface of Fino and Manzanilla sherry during the ageing process and which gives them their distinctive flavour.

**Fortified wine** a wine with a higher alcoholic strength than a table wine. Grape brandy is added at some stage during its production. Sherry and port are the most common examples.

**Franconia** German wine region, best for dry whites.

**Frascati** white DOC close to Rome.

**Frizzante** Italian for lightly sparkling wine.

**Fronsac** red AC of Bordeaux.

**Fumé Blanc** alternative name for Sauvignon Blanc in California and Australia, implying that the wine has been aged in oak.

**Gaillac** varied AC from southwest France.

**Gamay** the grape variety of Beaujolais. Also found in nearby appellations such as Côte Roannaise, and in the Loire valley and Savoie.

**Garrafeira** Portuguese term usually applied to the winemaker's best wine. The minimum requirements for red wines are two years ageing before bottling, followed by one year in bottle before sale; for white wine, six months ageing before bottling, followed by a further six months in bottle. The alcohol level must also be half a degree higher than the usual minimum for the area.

**Generoso** Spanish for a fortified dessert wine.

**Gewürztraminer** white grape variety making deliciously spicy wines, at its best in Alsace, but also found in the Alto Adige where it is said to have originated at the town of Tramin. It has travelled with some success to the New World. Gewürz means spice in German.

**Gisborne** wine region of New Zealand.

**Givry** red AC of the Côte Chalonnaise.

**Governo** a technique used in Tuscany for the production of some Chianti. This consists of adding must from 5–10 per cent of the grapes, which have been left to dry and concentrate, to vats of normally fermented wine, in order to cause refermentation. The aim is to make the wine ready for earlier drinking and is now used only by producers wishing to make a youthful style of Chianti.

**Gran Reserva** term used in Spain, especially in Rioja, for a wine which has been aged for a minimum of two years in oak cask and three in bottle, and released for sale in its sixth year. Only made in the very best years.

**Grand Cru** the best quality wine in several French appellations, notably in Alsace, Burgundy and parts of Bordeaux, where the best vineyards are described in this way.

**Grande Marque** term to describe the leading champagne houses, eg. Veuve Clicquot and Bolinger.

**Graves** red and white AC of Bordeaux.

**Grenache** a red grape of Spanish origin, where it is called Garnacha. In France it is widely grown in the Midi and the Rhône valley, notably for Châteauneuf-du-Pape. It makes heavy alcoholic wines which age quickly, so it is always blended with other varieties such as Syrah.

**Gris** French term for a pale pink wine, eg. Gris de Toul.

**Grosslage** *see* Germany.

**Halbtrocken** German description for medium dry wine, indicating the sugar level is not more than 10 g/l greater than the total acid content, with a maximum of 18 g/l. A Landwein must not be sweeter than halbtrocken. Qualitätswein may also be halbtrocken.

**Hawke's Bay** wine region of New Zealand.

**Hermitage** fine AC of northern Rhône.

**Hock** traditional English name for Rhine wine, possibly originating from the village Hochheim.

**Hunter Valley** important wine region of New South Wales.

**Imbottigliato da** Italian for bottled by.

**Individual Berry Selected** New World equivalent of Beerenauslese.

**Individual Bunch Selected** New World equivalent of Auslese.

**Invecchiato** on Italian labels describes a wine which has been matured for an unspecified time.

**Irancy** red AC of northern Burgundy.

**Jacquère** a grape grown extensively in Savoie which makes crisp dry white wine.

**Jeroboam** a bottle size equal to four ordinary bottles in Champagne (300 cl) and six in Bordeaux (450 cl).

**Jeunes Vignes** meaning 'young vines'; sometimes used to describe a wine made from vines too young for it to be included in the appellation.

**Juliénas** Beaujolais cru.

**Jumilla** fullbodied red DO of southern Spain.

**Jurançon** dry and sweet white wine of the Pyrenées.

**Kabinett** the lowest category of German Prädikat wine, made from grapes which are naturally ripe, so not requiring chaptalization. The term was first used at Kloster Eberbach by the Duke of Nassau, originally for particularly fine wines kept in a grower's private cellar or cabinet. Term also used in Austria, where Kabinett is not considered to be a Prädikat.

**Keller** German for a cellar.

**Kellerei** German for a winery.

**Kirmisi** Turkish for red.

**Kretzer** a pink wine in the Alto Adige. An alternative description to rosato in this German speaking part of the country.

**La Clape** part of Coteaux du Languedoc.

**Lalande de Pomerol** red Bordeaux AC close to Pomerol.

**Lambrusco** Italy's most popular wine, made from the grape of the same name.

Lightly sparkling, often sweet, usually red, occasionally pink or white.

**Landwein** *see* Germany.

**Laski Rizling** a synonym for Welschriesling.

**Late Bottled Vintage** or LBV describes a port which is aged longer in wood and bottled later than vintage port, between four and a half and six years after the vintage. It comes from a year not generally declared vintage.

**Late Harvest** New World term for Spätlese or Vendange Tardive, meaning that the grapes are picked later than the rest of the harvest and are therefore riper, making a sweeter wine.

**Les Baux** subregion of AC Coteaux d'Aix-en-Provence.

**Licoroso** Portuguese for fortified wine.

**Lie** or **Sur Lie** a term used particularly in relation to Muscadet, when the wine is bottled off the fine lees or sediment remaining from the fermentation. A little carbon dioxide remains and the wine retains its youthful, fresh fruitiness.

**Liebfraumilch** Germany's most popular wine abroad. The name literally means 'milk of Our Lady' and originates from the vineyard of the Liebfrauenkirche in Worms. Liebfraumilch must be a QbA wine and is produced mainly in the

Rheinpfalz and Rheingau from Müller–Thurgau, Silvaner, Kerner, Morio–Muscat and sometimes Riesling grapes.

**Lieblich** German for medium sweet.

**Liqueur d'Expédition** a mixture of wine, cane sugar and occasionally grape brandy which is added to a bottle of champagne after dégorgement.

**Liqueur Muscat** delicious Australian dessert wine.

**Liquoroso** Italian term for a dessert wine, which has been fortified with alcohol.

**Lirac** mainly red AC from southern Rhône.

**Listrac** Médoc AC.

**Long Island** up and coming vineyard area of New York State.

**Loupiac** sweet white Bordeaux AC.

**Lutomer** wine region of Yugoslavia.

**MA** on a champagne label indicates a marque auxiliaire or subsidiary brand, rather than the company's principal name.

**Macabeo** Spanish white grape variety, planted in Rioja and Penedés, and also in the south of France.

**Macération Carbonique** a relatively new vinification technique designed to produce fresh fruity red wines low in tannin and high in colour. Whole bunches of grapes are put into vats filled with carbon dioxide, when fermentation begins inside the grapes. Contrary to a normal fermentation, the pressed juice is a better quality than the free-run juice. This process is used particularly in Beaujolais and the Midi.

**Macharnudo** the best part of the sherry area, to the north of Jerez.

**Mâcon** *see* Burgundy.

**Madeira** *see* Fortified Wines.

**Madiran** up and coming red AC of southwest France.

**Maduro** or Vinho Maduro in Portuguese means a mature table wine as opposed to a young Vinho Verde.

**Magnum** a double bottle size–150 cl.

**Maipo** wine region of Chile.

**Málaga** fortified wine of Spain.

**Malbec** a less important grape in the Bordeaux blend, also grown in the Loire valley as Cot, and in Cahors as Auxerrois.

**Malmsey** the sweetest of the four types of madeira. The Duke of Clarence was drowned in a butt of Malmesy in Shakespeare's Richard III.

**Malolactic Fermentation** the secondary fermentation

which takes place after the main alcoholic fermentation. Malic acid, as in apples, is converted into lactic acid, as in milk, which reduces the total acidity of the wine. All red wines undergo a malolactic fermentation, but sometimes this is prevented in a white wine.

**Malvasia** a white grape variety, grown particularly in central Italy, but also found in other parts of Europe.

**Manzanilla** a distinctive type of sherry made only in Sanlúcar de Barrameda, with a particular salty tang, resulting from the wine's maturation by the sea.

**Margaret River** wine region of Western Australia.

**Margaux** AC of the Médoc and first growth château.

**Marlborough** wine region of New Zealand.

**Marsala** *see* Fortified Wines.

**Marsanne** the principal white grape variety of Hermitage in the northern Rhône.

**Maury** VDN of southern France.

**Mauzac** white grape variety grown in Gaillac and in the Aude for Blanquette de Limoux.

**Medium dry** a wine with a little residual sugar, but dry enough to drink during a meal.

**Medium sweet** a wine with a considerable amount of sugar, but not sweet enough to be a dessert wine.

**Médoc** important wine region of Bordeaux for claret.

**Mendocino** wine region of northern California.

**Mendoza** wine region of Argentina.

**Ménétou–Salon** AC of the Loire valley.

**Mercurey** AC of Côte Chalonnaise.

**Merlot** one of the principal grape varieties of Bordeaux, especially for Pomerol and St-Emilion, where it forms the larger proportion of the blend, with Cabernet Franc and Cabernet Sauvignon. It is also grown in northern Italy, eastern Europe and California.

**Messo in bottiglia** Italian for bottled.

**Méthode Champenoise** *see* Champagne method.

**Metodo Classico** Italian for champagne method.

**Millésime** French for vintage.

**Minervois** mainly red AC of the Midi.

**Mis en Bouteille** French for bottled.

**Moelleux** French for a soft rich wine, not necessarily very sweet. Common description for Vouvray.

**Monastrell** one of the most widely planted red grape varieties of Spain, especially in Alicante and Jumilla.

**Monbazillac** sweet white of southwest France.

**Montagny** white AC of Côte Chalonnaise.

**Montepulciano** a red grape variety grown in central and southern Italy, with no connection to Vino Nobile di Montepulciano.

**Montilla** sherry lookalike of southern Spain.

**Montlouis** dry to sweet and sparkling white AC of the Loire valley.

**Moscatel de Setúbal** dessert wine of Portugal.

**Moscato** Italian synonym for Muscat.

**Mosel–Saar–Ruwer** QbA of Germany.

**Morio–Muscat** aromatic German white wine grape variety, a cross between Silvaner and Pinot Gris.

**Moulis** AC of the Médoc.

**Mount Barker** wine region of Western Australia.

**Mourvèdre** red grape variety grown especially in Bandol, but also in the Midi, to give the wines more character.

**Mousseux** French for sparkling. Usually implies a wine made by the cuve close method.

**Muffa Nobile** Italian for noble rot.

**Müller–Thurgau** a popular German grape variety, a cross between a Riesling and Sylvaner, developed by a Doctor Müller in Thurgau.

**Muscadelle** white grape variety grown in southwest France, blended with Sémillon and Sauvignon to make sweet wine such as Sauternes.

**Muscadet** a white grape variety which makes the wine of the same name at the Atlantic end of the Loire valley.

**Muscat** there are several different types of Muscat. The best Muscat à Petits Grains makes the vins doux naturels of the south of France, such as Muscat de Beaumes-de-Venise. Muscat is grown all over Italy, in Alsace, California and Australia.

**Must** unfermented grape juice.

**Mutage** French term for stopping the fermentation, either by the addition of grape spirit, in order to make vin doux naturel or, by the use of sulphur dioxide and filtration, to leave some residual sugar for a sweet wine.

**NM** on a champagne label it means the wine has been made by a Négociant manipulant.

**Nahe** QbA of the Rhine.

**Naoussa** Greek wine region.

**Napa Valley** principal wine region of California.

**Naturwein** a term used in Austria to describe a wine made without chaptalization.

**Navarra** up and coming DO of northern Spain.

**Nebbiolo** the red grape variety grown in northwest Italy, making the finest wines of Piedmont, namely Barolo and Barbaresco.

**Négociant** a wine merchant in France who may own vineyards, but whose principal activity is to buy grapes, must and wine, which he blends and bottles to sell under his own name. A négociant–éleveur matures wines in his cellars and is responsible for the élèvage of the wine.

**Negramole** the most common grape variety of Madeira, used for blending.

**Nemea** Greek wine region.

**Niederösterreich** Austrian wine region.

**Nierstein** important Rheinhessen wine town.

**Noble Late Harvest** South African term to describe a wine made from grapes with noble rot, and with more than 50 g/l of sugar remaining after fermentation.

**Noble Rot** a condition caused by the fungus, *Botrytis cinerea*, which is responsible for the world's finest dessert wines. In the right climatic conditions of damp, misty autumnal mornings, followed by warm drying sunshine, the fungus attacks the skins of the ripe grapes, allowing their juice to concentrate, to make lusciously sweet wine.

**Non-vintage** term used to describe a wine sold without any mention of the year of harvest. Most common in champagne and port which are only sold as vintage in the best years. Otherwise they are a blend of years.

**Nouveau** French term for a new wine, sold in the autumn immediately after the vintage, and used most commonly in connection with Beaujolais. The description is generally valid until Christmas.

**Novello** Italian equivalent of nouveau.

**Novi Pazar** Bulgarian controlliran zone.

**Oechsle** the German system for estimating the potential alcohol content and quality of a wine. The reading of the must weight, by how much heavier it is than water, decides whether a wine will have a Prädikat.

**Oloroso** the darkest and richest sherry. It develops its character through ageing in wood. Unblended it is completely dry, but is often used as a base for Cream Sherry.

**Oppenheim** important Rheinhessen wine town.

**Oregon** wine producing state of northwest USA.

**Organic Wine** made from grapes cultivated without any chemical fertilizers, weedkillers or other treatments. In the cellar only the minimum use of sulphur is permitted.

**Originalabfüllung** German and Austrian for estate bottled.

**Orvieto** Italian white DOC from Umbria.

**Paarl** South African wine region.

**Palatinate** English name for Rheinpfalz.

**Pale Cream** tastes like cream sherry, while looking like Fino.

**Palette** tiny Provence AC.

**Palo Cortado** a maverick sherry which is neither quite an Amontillado or an Oloroso. It does not develop *flor* and ages well. Genuine Palo Cortado is very rare.

**Palomino** the principal grape variety for sherry.

**Parellada** one of the white grape varieties used for sparkling wine in Catalonia.

**Pasado** Spanish term used to describe fine old Fino and Amontillado.

**Paso Robles** Californian AVA.

**Passito** Italian for wine made from semi-dried grapes. The juice is rich and concentrated and the wine stronger and sweeter than normal.

**Patrimonio** Corsican AC.

**Pauillac** important Médoc AC.

**Pécharmant** red AC adjoining Bergerac.

**Pedro Ximénez** white grape variety grown all over Spain, especially for sherry and Montilla.

**Penedés** important northern Spanish wine region.

**Perlé** alternative to pétillant, as in Gaillac Perlé.

**Perlwein** cheap semi-sparkling wine in Germany.

**Pétillant** French for lightly sparkling wine.

**Phylloxera** a disease of the vine that devastated European viticulture at the end of the last century. An aphid, *Phylloxera vastatrix*, which attacks the roots of vines causing them to die, was inadvertently brought to France from America. The only remedy is to graft European vines on to phylloxera resistant American rootstock.

**Piesport** important Mosel wine village.

**Pinot Blanc** the white version of Pinot Noir, grown extensively in Alsace and northern Italy.

**Pinot Gris** a white grape

variety at its best in Alsace, where it can make Vendange Tardive wines in the best years. It is planted in grand cru vineyards. Also grown in Germany and northern Italy.

**Pinot Meunier** one of the principal red grape varieties used for champagne.

**Pinot Noir** the grape variety of fine red burgundy, and an important part of a champagne blend. Has adapted to the New World with less success as it is difficult to cultivate, requiring a long cool growing season. Probably at its best in Oregon, also found in Germany, northern Italy and eastern Europe.

**Pinotage** typical South African grape variety, a cross between Pinot Noir and Cinsaut.

**Podere** Italian for farm or estate.

**Pomerol** Bordeaux AC best known for Château Pétrus.

**Pouilly Fuissé** white Burgundy AC.

**Pouilly Fumé** dry white Loire AC.

**Pourriture Noble** French for noble rot.

**Prädikat** *see* Germany.

**Predicato** new classification of wines from central Tuscany. They are only table wines but have strict regulations covering four categories: Predicato di Cardisco based on

Sangiovese; Predicato di Biturica based on Cabernet Sauvignon; Predicato di Muschio based on Chardonnay and Predicato del Selvante based on Sauvignon.

**Primeur** or Vin de Primeur is a term almost synonymous with Nouveau.

**Propriétaire-Récoltant** on a French label it means the owner of the estate who harvested the grapes.

**Putt** indicates the degree of sweetness in Tokay. Three, four or five is usual and six is exceptional.

**Qualitätswein** *see* Germany.

**Quarts de Chaume** sweet white Loire.

**Quincy** dry white Loire AC.

**Quinta** Portuguese for a wine estate.

**RD** stands for Récemment Dégorgé, or recently disgorged. A term used by Bollinger for champagne which has been kept in their cellars under ideal conditions for several years until disgorged in readiness for sale and consumption.

**RM** on a champagne label stands for Récoltant Manipulant, meaning an individual grower.

**Rainwater** name used in Madeira to describe a light wine made from a blend of grapes. Stories about the dilution of the wine with rain account for the name.

**Rancio** the oxidized taste of fortified wine.

**Recioto** describes a Valpolicella or Soave made from dried grapes. The resulting wine may be sweet or dry but is usually a rich dessert wine. *See also* Amarone.

**Récolte** French for vintage.

**Remontage** essential part of red wine vinification, describing the process of pumping the fermenting juice over the cap of skins in the vat in order to extract colour and tannin.

**Remuage** part of the méthode champenoise process designed to facilitate the removal of sediment resulting from the second fermentation in the bottle. The bottles are placed horizontally in *pupitres* (racks) and twisted a little every day, so that by the end the sediment rests on the cork of the upside down bottle.

**Reserva** in Portugal describes a wine of outstanding quality with a vintage. It must have half a degree higher than normal alcohol, but the precise ageing depends upon the grower's decision. In Spain reserva indicates that the wine has been aged for a minimum of one year in cask and released in its fourth year. Only made in good years.

**Réserve** term on a French label, sometimes qualified by Personnelle, Exceptionelle, etc., to denote a wine the producer considers to be better than average.

**Reserve Bin Number X** Australian term for a special wine, identified by number.

**Reuilly** Loire AC.

**Rheingau** one of the finest QbA's of Germany.

**Rheinhessen** QbA of Germany's Rhineland.

**Rheinpfalz** QbA of Germany's Rhineland.

**Ribeiro** Spanish DO for dry white wine.

**Ribetejo** Portuguese wine area.

**Ried** Austrian for vineyard.

**Riesling Italico** *see* Welschriesling.

**Riesling** the white grape variety which makes all Germany's finest wines. It is susceptible to noble rot and, in the best years, can produce deliciously honeyed Auslese wines and even better. Also grown successfully in the New World, where the wines tend to be fuller and higher in alcohol. Likewise in Alsace it is fermented dry, except when Vendange Tardive and Sélection de Grains Nobles are made.

**Rioja** important Spanish DO.

**Riserva** Italian term for a wine which has been aged for longer than usual in barrel, and possibly also in bottle, and is, therefore, a better vintage and quality than the basic DOC wine.

**Riserva Speciale** Italian term to describe a wine which has been aged longer in barrel, and maybe in bottle, than a riserva wine and is of even better quality.

**Rivesaltes** VDN from the Midi.

**Rosado** Spanish and Portuguese for pink.

**Rosato** Italian for pink.

**Rosé** French for pink.

**Rosso** Portuguese, Spanish and Italian for red.

**Rotling** German for pink wine.

**Rotwein** German for red wine.

**Rouge** French for red.

**Roussanne** a white grape variety of the Rhône, best with Marsanne for Hermitage. Also found in Savoie and Montecarlo in Tuscany.

**Roussette** white grape grown in Savoie for AC Roussette de Savoie; also grown in Bugey.

**Ruby** describes a basic young port, deep in colour, which has been aged in wood for only two or three years.

**Rueda** Spanish DO for white wine.

**Ruländer** German name for Pinot Gris.

**Rully** AC of Côte Chalonnaise.

**Rutherglen** Australian wine region known for Liqueur Muscat, made from overripe grapes.

**Ružica** Yugoslav for pink.

**St-Chinian** part of the Coteaux du Languedoc.

**St-Croix-du-Mont** sweet white Bordeaux AC.

**St-Emilion** important red Bordeaux AC.

**St-Estèphe** important Médoc AC.

**St-Joseph** northern Rhône AC.

**St-Julien** important Médoc AC.

**St-Péray** still and sparkling white Rhône AC.

**St-Pourçain** upper Loire VDQS.

**St-Véran** white southern Burgundy AC.

**Sancerre** popular Loire AC.

**Sangiovese** red grape variety grown all over central Italy. A vital ingredient of Chianti, at its best in Brunello di Montalcino. An inferior version makes Sangiovese di Romagna.

**Santa Ynez Valley** Californian AVA.

**Sarap** Turkish for wine.

**Saumur** centre for sparkling Loire wine; also AC for still wine.

**Sauternes** delicious sweet wine from Bordeaux.

**Sauvignon** white grape variety making crisp white wines in the central Loire, as well as in southwest France where it is sometimes blended with Sémillon. Has travelled successfully to the New World, where it is sometimes aged in oak and called Fumé Blanc.

**Savagnin** distinctive white grape variety of Jura, responsible for Vin Jaune.

**Savennières** distinctive dry white Loire AC.

**Schaumwein** German for sparkling wine, without any specific quality or origin.

**Scheurebe** German grape variety, a cross between Silvaner and Riesling.

**Schloss** German for castle.

**Secco** Italian for dry.

**Seco** Portuguese and Spanish for dry.

**Sekt** German for sparkling wine, but better quality than Schaumwein. Deutscher Sekt now means that the base wine comes from Germany, where the second fermentation also takes place. If a more precise region of origin is given, only 85% of the grapes need come from that area. The same applies to grape variety and vintage. The most common method of production is cuve close.

**Sélection de Grains Nobles** Alsace term to describe a wine made from grapes which are particularly ripe and affected by noble rot. Only Muscat, Pinot Gris, Riesling or Gewürztraminer may be used. Such wine is made only in the very best years.

**Sémillon** the principal grape variety for Sauternes and other sweet wines of southwest France, since it is particularly susceptible to noble rot. Also important in the Graves for oak aged, dry white wines. In Australia's Hunter Valley it makes some of the country's most distinctive white wines.

**Sercial** the driest style of madeira.

**Seyssel** Savoie AC for still and sparkling wine.

**Shiraz** Australian and South African synonym for Syrah.

**Show Reserve** Australian term to describe award winning wine at the national wine show.

**Silvaner** white grape variety, at one time planted widely in Germany, and now being superseded by Müller–Thurgau. Makes interesting wine in Franconia and is also grown in Alsace.

**Soave** northern Italian dry white DOC.

**Solera** ageing system for

sherry and madeira. The barrels are arranged in a series of scales, containing the same wine, with each scale younger than the last. As wine is drawn off from the oldest barrels, it is replaced by some slightly younger wine, and so on down the scale. The solera system depends upon the fact that the younger wine quickly takes on the character of the older wine.

**Somontano** Spanish red DO.

**Sonoma** important wine region of California.

**Sparkling wine** general term describing a wine containing bubbles of carbon dioxide, usually originating from a second fermentation.

**Spätburgunder** German name for Pinot Noir.

**Spätlese** second category of German Prädikat wines, meaning late picked. The grapes are picked at least seven days after the start of the harvest for the particular grape variety, so that they are richer in sugar. Also used in Austria.

**Special Late Harvest** South African category describing a wine between Late Harvest and Noble Late Harvest with 20–30 g/l of sugar.

**Spitzenwein** Austrian equivalent of German Prädikat wine.

**Spumante** sparkling wine in Italy.

**Steen** South African name for Chenin Blanc.

**Steiermark** Austrian wine region.

**Stellenbosch** South African wine region.

**Still wine** a table wine without any carbon dioxide to make it fizzy.

**Stravecchio** Italian for very old.

**Suhindol** Bulgarian wine region.

**Sulphur Dioxide** important in both vineyard and cellars. In the vineyard it is used to treat disease and in the cellar it acts as an antiseptic, eliminating wild yeast and harmful bacteria. It also prevents oxidation and can be used to stop a fermentation.

**Supérieur** French term denoting an extra degree of alcohol above the basic appellation, and sometimes a smaller yield.

**Superiore** Italian term denoting a wine with more alcohol, eg. Frascati superiore, or longer ageing, eg. Valpolicella superiore.

**Süss** German for sweet.

**Svichtov** Bulgarian Controliran zone.

**Syrah** the red grape variety of the northern Rhône, responsible for fine wines such as Hermitage and Côte Rôtie. Also grown in the Midi, to improve the region's traditional wines, and successfully in Australia as Shiraz.

**Szurkebarat** Hungarian name for Pinot Gris, translating literally as 'grey monk'.

**Tannin** a vital component of red wine, particularly essential in any wine destined for ageing. It comes from the skins, pips and stalks of grapes and in a young wine is detected by a puckering sensation in the mouth, not unlike the effect of strong tea. As the wine matures, the tannin softens.

**Tartrates** crystals of tartaric acid that develop in a wine when subjected to extremely cold temperature. To prevent this occurring in the bottle, a wine may be given cold stabilization treatment before bottling.

**Tavel** pink AC of southern Rhône.

**Tawny Port** a blend of wines from different years, matured in wood until they are ready for drinking. The colour turns tawny with age. Twenty year old tawny is made from wines with an average age of twenty years. Cheap tawny is often a blend of red and white port.

**Tempranillo** most important and finest red grape variety of Rioja, also grown in Navarre and Valdepeñas.

**Tenuta** Italian for farm or estate, often part of an estate name.

**Tinto** Spanish for deep red wine, as opposed to a clarete. Also describes red wine in Portugal.

**Tokay** Hungary's finest dessert wine and also a synonym for Pinot Gris in Alsace. Its use as such is disputed by the EEC authorities.

**Torgiano** DOC of Umbria.

**Toro** red DO of Spain.

**Touraine** Loire AC best for Sauvignon.

**Transfer Method** a method of making sparkling wine that is a cross between the cuve close and champagne methods. The second fermentation takes place in the bottle, but in order to avoid the processes of remuage and dégorgement, the wine is transferred back into the vat for filtering and bottling.

**Transvasage** another name for the transfer method.

**Trebbiano** uninspiring white grape variety grown extensively in Italy; a vital ingredient of wines such as Soave, Orvieto, Frascati, etc. In southern France it is called Ugni Blanc and features in most of the region's white wines. Needs to be blended with something else for flavour. It is also distilled for armagnac and cognac.

**Trocken** German for dry. A new legal description for wines with less than 4 g/l of sugar. A current fashion.

**Trockenbeerenauslese** the sweetest category of German Prädikat wines, meaning literally a selection of dried berries. The grapes are so affected by noble rot that they become like raisins and make lusciously sweet wines, with low alcohol. Only made in exceptional years.

**Ugni blanc** French synonym for Trebbiano.

**Uvaggio** Italian for grape varieties.

**VSR–Vin Sans Récolte** sometimes found on a French label to indicate a non-vintage wine.

**Vacqueyras** village of the southern Rhône.

**Valpolicella** popular northern Italian red.

**Varietal** American term for a grape variety, increasingly used to describe a wine predominantly made from one variety.

**Vecchio** Italian for old; can refer to a specific ageing period for some wines.

**Velha** Portuguese for old, with specified amount of ageing before sale.

**Vendange Tardive** French for Late Harvest. The term describes a quality of wine made in Alsace from Riesling, Pinot Gris, Muscat or Gewürztraminer in better years only.

**Verdelho** a style of madeira, sweeter than Sercial and drier than Bual.

**Verdicchio** Italian grape variety making white wine of the same name, sometimes blended with Trebbiano and Malvasia.

**Vernaccia** Italian grape variety at its most typical in the white Vernaccia di San Gimignano. Another white version is grown in Sardinia and a red variety near Ancona.

**Verwaltung** a German term meaning administration.

**VIDE** the Associazione Viticinicoltori Italiani, a voluntary organization of about 30 winemakers from all over Italy. Wines which pass their strict self-imposed tasting tests are sold with the VIDE neck label.

**Vieilles Vignes** literally 'old vines' in French. Older vines produce better wine because their root systems are more developed. Their grapes are sometimes vinified and sold separately as a special cuvée.

**Vigna** Italian for vineyard.

**Vigneron** French for a winemaker.

**Vigneto** Italian for vineyard.

**Vignoble** French for vineyard.

**Vin de Consommation Courante** French for basic table wine.

**Vin de Corse** principal AC of Corsica.

**Vin de Paille** literally 'straw wine'. So called because the grapes are traditionally dried on straw after the harvest. They become raisin-like with rich concentrated juice to make sweet, rich wine. A speciality of the Jura.

**Vin de Pays** *see* France.

**Vin de Pays de l'Ile de Beauté** basic wine of Corsica.

**Vin de Pays du Jardin de la France** wine from the whole Loire valley.

**Vin de Savoie** principal AC of Savoie.

**Vin de Table** *see* France.

**Vin de Tête** term used in Sauternes to describe a wine from the first and therefore best pressing. Crème de Tête is even better, from the very ripest grapes.

**Vin Délimité de Qualité Supérieure** *see* France.

**Vin Doux Naturel (VDN)** literally 'naturally sweet wine'. Fortified wine from the south of France, such as Muscat de Beaumes-de-Venise. The fermentation is stopped by the addition of alcohol so that the wine is rich in natural sugar.

**Vin du Bugey** principal wine of Bugey.

**Vin d'une Nuit** a pink wine, for which the juice has spent just one night in contact with the skins to obtain the necessary colour.

**Vin Jaune** a speciality of the Jura, made from the

Savagnin grape. The wine is aged in barrels, which are never topped up, for a minimum of six years so that a *flor* develops which gives the wine a distinctive flavour.

**Vin Nature** French for a dry wine without any added sugar, and in Champagne a still wine.

**Vin Ordinaire** another term for basic vin de table.

**Vin Santo** traditional Tuscan dessert wine. The grapes are left to dry and then ferment very slowly in small barrels, which are sealed for as long as six years.

**Vina** Spanish for vineyard, but used rather loosely on a label.

**Vinedos Proprios** South American for own vineyards.

**Vinho** Portuguese for wine.

**Vinho de Mesa** Portuguese for table wine.

**Vinho Verde** light white Portuguese wine; also means young wine.

**Vino** Italian and Spanish for wine.

**Vino da Tavola** *see* Italy.

**Vino Nobile di Montepulciano** Tuscan red DOCG, similar to Chianti.

**Vintage** term used to describe the harvest of the grapes; also refers to the year of the wine.

# GLOSSARY

**Vintage Character** good quality ruby port, a blend of several years, aged in wood for four or five years. As the name implies it is not dissimilar to a true vintage port in style.

**Vintage Port** not to be confused with Late Bottled Vintage. This is a wine made in exceptional years, bottled after two years in wood and intended for further ageing.

**Viognier** distinctive white grape of the northern Rhône, at its best in Condrieu and Château Grillet, typified by a flavour of apricots.

**Vitigno** Italian for grape variety.

**Voros** Hungarian for red.

**Vouvray** Loire AC for dry to sweet, still and sparkling white wine.

**Washington State** wine producing state of northwest USA.

**Wein** German for wine.

**Weingut** German for wine estate. The term may only appear on the label if the wine comes exclusively from that estate.

**Weissherbst** very pale pink German wine made especially in Baden.

**Weisswein** German for white wine.

**Welschriesling** not to be confused with Rhine Riesling. A grape variety grown extensively in eastern Europe for undistinguished quaffable white wine, such as Lutomer Laski Rizling.

**Wine of Origin** the South African equivalent of Appellation Contrôlée, with 17 defined Regions of Origin.

**Winery** New World term for the place where a wine is made; also describes a wine making company.

**Winzergenossenschaft** a growers' cooperative in Germany.

**Wood Matured** New World term to describe a wine which has been aged in wood before bottling. It usually means new oak.

**Wood Port** term to describe port blended and aged in cask until ready for drinking.

**Xarel-lo** white grape variety grown in Penedés for Cava.

**Xynisteri** white grape variety of Cyprus.

**Xynomavro** important red grape variety in Greece.

**Zibibbo** Muscat grape variety grown on Pantelleria.

**Zinfandel** most distinctive grape variety of California. Makes a wide range of wine styles from pale pink and nouveau through to hefty Late Harvest port styles. Fullbodied berry-flavoured reds are best.